Intoduction to News Writing
The Real Scoop

Second Edition

Kathryn Quigley
Rowan University

Kendall Hunt
publishing company

www.kendallhunt.com
Send all inquiries to:
4050 Westmark Drive
Dubuque, IA 52004-1840

Copyright © 2006, 2012 by Kathryn Quigley

ISBN 978-1-4652-0393-9

Printed in the United States of America
10 9 8 7 6 5 4 3 2

To my son, Nicholas Robert Quigley.
You bring joy to my life every day.
I love you.

Contents

Preface

So many things changed in technology, the world and journalism since I wrote the first edition of this textbook in 2006.

The Middle East experienced the "Arab Spring" of reform. Twitter and Facebook gained social media users at an explosive rate. Newspapers, magazines and TV news programs continued to change and restructure.

But one thing remains the same: the need for compelling and concise news stories. Now, more than ever, journalists need to be able to get the stories right. And they need to write and report faster than ever.

"Introduction to News Writing: The Real Scoop" is designed to help college journalism students and those just starting out in the field to gain knowledge and confidence.

There are a lot of dense academic books out there about journalism. This isn't one of them. Throughout my career as a newspaper reporter, freelance journalist and journalism professor, I learned to write in a spare, precise and often humorous way. That's how I wrote this textbook.

Inside these pages, you will find detailed advice and tips on how to cover typical journalism assignments, plus interviews with top reporters and editors. Each chapter contains Ten Tips, plus tear-out assignments to be completed as homework. Good luck and thanks for reading.

Chapter 1
The Basics

Courtesy of Jesse Bair

To tell a story, you have to start at the very beginning. To tell a journalistic story, you need to start with the basics. Once you master all the elements of basic journalistic writing, you can craft compelling and interesting stories. But it takes work and a lot of practice. Becoming a great journalist, and not just a mediocre one, takes time.

Think of a news story as a cake – you need to gather the ingredients, mix them correctly and bake them for the right amount of time for it to be done. And edible.

There are three main ingredients to any kind of journalism story: the LEAD (sometimes spelled lede), the NUTGRAPH and the KICKER.

The LEAD is the very beginning of the story or news broadcast. It is the first thing the audience reads, sees or hears. It must be correct, concise and sometimes clever.

Here is a lead from Lane DeGregory of the St. Petersburg Times about a kind-hearted mailman.

On his day off, the mailman returns to his route.

He drives a beat-up Cherokee with a homemade trailer hitched to the bumper, parks in front of the little blue house on a corner lot tangled with weeds.

He carries no mailbag. He has nothing to deliver. Except his time.

DeGregory, an award-winning writer, goes on to describe how the mailman cuts the lawns of all the elderly residents along his route. A lazy journalist (or one with not much talent) might have written a lead like this:

"A Florida mailman mows the lawn of senior citizens on his day off."

Snore. What is clever or interesting about that? Leads must grab readers and hold their interest.

In 1995, a South Carolina mother went on trial for the drowning of her two little boys, whom she claimed had been carjacked. It was a lie. Rick Bragg reported on the story for the New York Times and covered the murder trial and murder conviction of Susan Smith. This is his lead from the subsequent murder trial story about Smith's sentencing:

A jury today decided that Susan Smith should not be put to death for the drowning of her two young sons and instead should spend the rest of her life in prison, remembering.

The key to the lead, in my opinion, is the comma after the word "prison." It allows the reader to pause and think about the dead little boys and how their mother would spend the rest of her life with their memories and the horror of what she did.

After a great lead, a story needs a NUTGRAPH. That is a paragraph or sentence that sums up the entire story. The nutgraph must go up high in a news story – at least by the fifth paragraph or so. It can be delayed in a feature story. The purpose of the nutgraph is to quickly sum up the story so that the reader or viewer can get the gist of the story quickly. After the nutgraph, the story can continue chronologically. Forgetting to write a nutgraph is one of the most common mistakes made by beginning journalism students. Here is the nutgraph in the Susan Smith sentencing story:

"It took the jury two and one-half hours to reject the prosecution's request for the death penalty and settle on a life sentence. The jury's unanimous decision saved Mrs. Smith, 25, from death row, but left her alone in a tiny cell with the ghosts of her dead children, for at least the next 30 years."

Once the story is written, the reporter must focus on the KICKER. That is the very last sentence or paragraph of a story or broadcast. It is the last thing a reader will grasp before the story is done. Don't just let the story trail off – save a really good quote or detail for the kicker. Here's another tip – write the kicker first and then go back and write the story. But whatever you do, make sure that there is something interesting at the very end of your story. Don't just suddenly...stop.

Here is the next set of "ingredients" needed to create a successful news story: Who, What, Why, When, Where and How. This sounds rather basic and it is. But too often beginning journalism students overlook these important elements.

Say that you are doing a story for the college newspaper about a student government meeting and a proposed tuition hike. A reporter needs to get ALL the details and include them in the story, or else it simply won't be complete.

- **WHO:** The students at the college. The student government officers.

- **WHAT:** A meeting to discuss a tuition hike.

- **WHY:** Students need to know the specifics of why the tuition increase is needed. Is the money going to build a new football stadium? Are there less students enrolling? Is it because of a faltering economy?

- **WHEN:** Let readers or viewers know when the meeting occurred. Make sure to explain the exact time frame of the tuition increase.

- **WHERE:** Don't forget to name the college.

- **HOW:** Get the specifics on how much money the tuition increase will raise (revenue) and how much the college will spend (expenditures). Give students information about student loans if they need additional financial aid.

All stories – even ones about college tuition hikes – need QUOTES from people involved. Readers and viewers want to know what other people think. They want to know what officials and experts think about a certain subject. This is where quotes come in.

The most important thing for a reporter to remember that a quote is what is said EXACTLY as it comes out of the person's mouth and is written down verbatim. Only then can it be called a quote. If you are just writing down the gist of what a person says, but not the exact words, then that is known as "paraphrasing."

It is important to distinguish quotes from other information in your notes. Mark the quotes with quotation marks or underline them. Do NOT mix them all together and hope you will remember later. If you are writing a story that requires the submission of your notes to an editor or fact checker, be aware that the quotes must be identified as such.

Here is a good quote from Lane DeGregory's story about the helpful mailman, Eric Wills:

"A yard is a reflection of the person who lives here," Wills says. "So why not help them feel better?"

The quote helps to illuminate the story and explain Wills' motivation. It is important to note the punctuation around the quotation. Use quotation marks at the beginning of the quote, a comma at the end of the phrase, then quotation marks again. The comma goes INSIDE the quotation mark. The attribution (he says or he said) goes at the end of the quote – not at the beginning.

Here is a quote from the story of the sentencing of convicted murderer Susan Smith, after she was sentenced to life in prison for killing her two little boys:

"This young woman is in a lake of fire," said (her) lawyer, David Bruck. "That's her punishment."

Once again, the quote adds context to a very sad story.

Some beginning journalists are very shy or lack confidence in talking to prominent people, like defense attorneys or politicians. Instead of doing the interview in person or on the phone, they try to conduct their interviews completely through email. DO NOT DO THIS.

First of all, it is really inefficient. Most people get so much email that the message from you could get lost in the shuffle. Secondly, email interviews don't convey either tone or context.

The best way to do an interview or get quotes is in person, with a phone interview the next best way. If you are nervous, picture yourself as a super hero – Reporter Gal or Reporter Guy. You can even have a cape. Reporter Guy and Gal are confident and talented. They can handle any interview.

Also, write down questions and notes before you pick up the phone or interview someone in person. Make sure you have researched the subject so you will be knowledgeable. If you don't understand what the person tells you, ASK QUESTIONS. It is okay to do so.

A reporter gets quotes by asking questions and listening to the response. Try not to do all the talking. Make sure you get the person's first and last name (make sure they spell it) and their job title, if it is relevant. Often, an editor will want you to get the person's age or hometown as well.

The best ideas are ones that journalists come up with themselves. Some story ideas will be assigned to you, but most will come from your own reporting and knowing the beat. If you are covering the local high school's baseball team for a weekly newspaper, you would get to know the names of the coaches and players, plus their statistics and game schedule. Therefore, you would know that the team making the state playoffs would be a good story.

But what IS news and how do journalists know when something is a story? They assess the NEWS VALUES – the elements involved which determine if something is worth reporting on:

- **TIMELINESS**: Did it happen recently? Remember it is called "news" and not "olds."

- **IMPACT**: Will affect many people? A hurricane has a lot of impact and so does a tax increase for the middle class.

- **PROXIMITY**: An event that happens nearby. For a local weekly newspaper, that means news in that county or town. For a large daily newspaper, this News Value expands out to a large city area or region.

- **PROMINENCE**: If someone famous or notable is involved, the story is most likely news – even if the action isn't that important.

- **CONFLICT**: Wars, riots, sports rivalries and political clashes are all examples of conflict

- **ODDITY**: Is it weird, funny or just plain strange?

- **VOICE TO THE VOICELESS**: Sometimes a story is news simply because it is happening to a marginalized member of society. It is a journalist's job to give "voice to the voiceless," as spelled out in the Society of Professional Journalists' Code of Ethics. This means stories about immigrants, the homeless, mentally ill, abused children etc.

Once a reporter has done all the reporting and interviewing, it is time to write. The best way to combat nerves or writer's block is to create a computer file or document. Immediately start writing your most vivid impressions of what you just learned. Don't even look at your notebook.

Now, go through all your notes and create a system to organize them. Highlight the quotes, for instance or put a star next to an important fact. Think of good ideas for the lead, nutgraph and kicker. Do NOT sit there staring at a blank screen. Do NOT sit there waiting for the perfect lead to fall out of the sky. It won't. It is perfectly acceptable to start in the middle and write down, or start at the bottom and do the lead last. There are no rules, as long as the story gets finished and has structure.

Here is a good way to give structure to a story. I learned this at a writing conference from Rick Bragg, the former New York Times reporter who now teaches journalism in Alabama. It is called the FIVE BOX OUTLINE. Here it is:

Box 1:   The LEAD. A good quote. First major point. Important details.

Box 2:   The nutgraph. Second major point. More details. Another anecdote or quote(s).

Box 3:   Third major point. Details. Boring But Important (statistics, facts, figures).

Box 4:   Fourth major point. Details. Quotes.

Box 5:   Wrap it up. The kicker.

Connect all the boxes with transitional words, like "and," "meanwhile" or "next" and the story will come together. Outlines make the writing easier and the Five Box Outline is easy to follow.

10 Tips on *Mastering the Basics*

- Write a great **lead**, **nutgraph** and **kicker**.
- Make sure you sufficiently answered **Who**, **What**, **Why**, **When**, **Where** and **How**.
- Determine what makes the story news: **Timeliness, Impact, Proximity, Prominence, Conflict, Oddity, Voice to the Voiceless**.
- Make sure the story is **fair**, **balanced** and **accurate**.
- Get enough **quotes** from enough people.
- If you don't understand, ask more **questions** and do more **research**.
- **Discuss** the story with your editor before you turn it in.
- If you are nervous talking to strangers, pretend you are **Reporter Gal** or **Reporter Guy**, complete with a cape.
- Don't be lazy and do the interview by e-mail. Pick up the **phone** or better yet, go in **person**.
- Know that you will make mistakes. But if you **correct them** and **learn from them**, that will make you a better journalist.

In-Class Activity/Homework

Get a news article from a newspaper, magazine or website.

What is the LEAD?

_____

What is the NUTGRAPH?

_____

What is the KICKER?

_____

WHO _____

WHAT _____

WHY _____

WHEN _____

WHERE _____

HOW _____

What NEWS VALUES are in the story?

_____

Now look through another newspaper, magazine or website. Write a LEAD that you like:

_____

Write a LEAD that is dull, boring or too complicated:

_____

Look for QUOTES.

Journalist Q&A

Courtesy of Jason Alt

Charles W. Nutt

Where did you work?

Various Gannett newspapers in New Jersey and New York for 36 years. New York Times for a year and a half.

What was your beat or job title?

Primarily Editor and Publisher for Gannett newspapers. Copy editor on the metropolitan desk for the NY Times.

Where did you go to college and what was your degree?

B.A. in English from the University of Scranton and M.A. in journalism from Syracuse University. Davenport Fellowship in Economics Reporting at the University of Missouri.

Did you work on your college newspaper or online news website?

Managing editor of college newspaper. (No website in those days. No computers, in fact. Manual typewriters. And the printing company set copy on Linotype machines.)

Did you have any internships? If so, where and what did you do?

No internships, but a graduate assistantship at Syracuse, working as editor of newsletters and then a magazine for the New York State Publishers Association and the New York Press Association.

When and where was your first journalism job? What is one thing you learned from it?

Hired as a night suburban reporter for The Courier-News (Gannett Co.) in Bridgewater, NJ. I quickly learned that it's good to be tall. Those were the days when reporters had to type stories on sheets of paper (with two carbon copies) and then paste the sheets together in a roll. The night editor's rule for story length was that when you held the story at arm's length and let it unroll, it shouldn't touch the floor. That meant I got to write longer stories (I'm six feet tall) than my friend the police reporter (who was 5-foot-6).

What was the hardest part of your first journalism job?

Knocking on the door of a home where the son had just been murdered and asking the family members for a photo and information.

Many beginning journalists get very nervous about their first assignments. Did you get nervous and how did you cope?

No, surprisingly, I never felt nervous. Almost the opposite. I'm basically an introvert, so I had to become in effect a different person – sort of what I assume an actor does when taking on a new role.

What is the worst part about being a journalist?

Long, bad and unpredictable hours that were often out of sync with the schedules of my wife and four kids.

What is the best part?

Feeling that what you do makes a difference in the lives of individual people and the community at large.

What advice would you give to a journalism major?

I always told prospective hires that getting ahead in the news business is often a matter of luck, but you can put yourself in a position to be lucky. You do that by taking advantage of every opportunity that comes along. Try new things, whether you want to or not. You sometimes discover new skills or new interests that way. Then when a new opportunity opens up, you're in a position to know whether you would like it or not, and you can point to the experience you have had. I think that advice is especially good today when it's absolutely imperative for new journalists to be able to work in print and all forms of digital platforms.

What would you tell yourself at the beginning of your career, if you could go back in time?

Put more money into the 401-k :-)

Chapter 2
School and Government

Courtesy of Paul Lutes III

Many journalists begin their careers by covering school board and government meetings. The process of government can be confusing. City council members use words like "millage" and "ordinance." They vote on issues that seem odd, like reports from the "Shade Tree Committee."

School board meetings can be even worse. The superintendent, school board members and teachers can get really focused on test scores, FTEs and pedagogy. If it sounds like a foreign language, that is actually kind of the point.

In the United States, government and school officials are required to conduct business in public. But that doesn't mean they will do it in a way that the average person can understand. That is your job as a reporter. You cover the school board meeting so that the single working mother doesn't have to attend. You write about the city council's plan to raise taxes because it will affect the senior citizens who live on fixed incomes.

Government and education reporters have to cover meetings as part of their beats. Meetings are useful because that is where action takes place. Taxes are raised or lowered. New high schools are built. The Ku Klux Klan gets approval – or rejection – for their request to parade through town.

The trouble is, meetings can be long and confusing. But the more meetings a reporter covers, the easier they are to write about. School board and government meetings are where news happens.

First, find the website for the town or school board and find out when and where the meeting is. Write down or print out the name of the mayor and city council members. For a school board meeting, find out the names of the superintendent and the board members.

Next, get there early. Doing so allows reporters to introduce themselves to the city clerk or secretary. This is important for checking votes and name spellings. Say hello to the city manager and mayor, or the superintendent and school board president if you've got time. Sit where you can see and hear. Don't hide but don't draw attention either.

Of course, once you have been covering a particular town or school board for a while, then the officials already know you. In that case, make sure you prepare for the meeting by reading the agenda ahead of time and doing some preliminary interviews. The agenda is your road map for what will happen during the meeting. Keep a sharp eye for any last-minute additions to the agenda – sometimes board members like to sneak these in to avoid media attention.

Pay attention to who is speaking. Create a code for your notes; for example, write "P" at the top of each quote made by the president of the school board. Keep your ears open when members of the community speak during public comment. You MUST get their names. It is not okay to write, "A resident complained." People have to state their names before they speak. Go up to them afterwards to double-check the spelling.

Another point to remember is that government and education types like to speak in jargon. Do not be afraid to ask them what they mean. Remember to keep the jargon out of your stories, too.

Think about how you're going to file your story on a late deadline, and prepare before the meeting if possible. Have a backup plan.

Remember there are two sides to every issue. Be sure to get each side, whether it is two factions of the school board fighting with each other or environmentalists upset with developers about new home construction.

Even if it is late, stay afterwards to get quotes from board members on the issue you're writing about. You want different and fresh quotes than the ones all the other newspapers will have. This is also the time to ask questions about issues you don't understand.

Do not write a chronological story: "First the council said the Pledge of Allegiance, then approved the minutes of the last meeting, then heard a progress report on the Elm Avenue Streetscaping Tax Increment Financing Proposal ... then after public comment...blah, blah, blah." Lead with the most important thing.

If the issue AFFECTS A LOT OF PEOPLE or COSTS A LOT OF MONEY, that's what will be the most important news from the meeting

When members of the public speak, go to them immediately and ask for their name, how it's spelled, where they're from. Do this while they're still sitting in the audience. Don't wait for the end of the meeting because you might never find them again. Quoting some anonymous "person who attended the meeting" is really lame.

Know the public records law in your state. Know which issues – and which issues only – boards can discuss in private. Challenge the school board or government body if they try to bar you from a meeting that you know to be open. Be prepared to cite your state's public records law.

Topics Often Discussed in City Council Meetings

- Taxes

- Road improvements

- Salaries of public safety and city workers

- Budgets

- New construction

- Snow removal

- Personnel issues (hiring and firing)

- Crime

- Water and sewer issues
- Politics

Topics Often Discussed at School Board Meetings

- Test scores
- New schools
- Bus routes
- Personnel issues (hiring and firing)
- Taxes
- Budget
- Curriculum (classes and concepts)

When Covering a Meeting, Always Write Down

- Actions taken (Did they APPROVE, DENY or TABLE a motion to do something?)
- Who voted and how
- The size of the audience
- Length of the meeting (if very short or long)
- Quotes from the board members
- Quotes from the public
- Political parties of the board members
- Background/details of the topics discussed

Here is some good writing from Kristen A. Graham, education reporter for The Philadelphia Inquirer. In the Aug. 25, 2011 edition, she wrote about a tense and often bizarre meeting after the superintendent of the Philadelphia School District took a buyout of her contract and resigned. The school district is run by a group called the Philadelphia School Reform Commission. Many in the crowd were unhappy and angry about the departure of Superintendent Arlene Ackerman. One audience member carried a staff, another sang a song and there were chants and catcalls.

Outrage over Ackerman's buyout erupts at SRC meeting

The Philadelphia Inquirer

Aug. 25, 2011

Kristen A. Graham, Staff Writer

Outrage at the Philadelphia School Reform Commission bubbled over Wednesday when it unanimously approved a buyout approaching $1 million for former Superintendent Arlene C. Ackerman.

The commission did not offer comment, answer questions, or discuss the controversial package at the raucous racially and politically charged meeting.

Ackerman's payment includes $905,000 - from $500,000 in district funds and $405,000 in private, anonymous donations funneled through a nonprofit with ties to the Philadelphia School District.

She will also get health and life insurance through June 2013 and an additional check for the value of her unused sick and vacation time, it was disclosed Wednesday. A district spokesman said he did not know the dollar value of the insurance or the sick and vacation time.

Some at the meeting said Ackerman's fate was in part the result of racial tensions.

Ackerman was "lynched" by politicians and the SRC "carried the rope," said Leon Williams, a lawyer and activist.

Her crime, Williams said, "was, she did not kiss the rumps of the politicians. And that she gave too large a contract to a black vendor," referring to a controversial $7.5 million contract for surveillance cameras.

Many of the more than 100 people in attendance at Wednesday's meeting booed when the commission members entered the auditorium, setting the tone for a wild and often uncomfortable meeting.

One speaker led a spontaneous version of the song "The Greatest Love of All." Another suggested that Tuesday's earthquake happened because the SRC had bought out Ackerman.

"Shame, shame, shame," some cried. "All of them must go!" people shouted when the vote to approve Ackerman's deal was over.

When one speaker said the next superintendent should not earn as much as Ackerman, whose base salary was $348,140, the audience erupted in shouts and catcalls.

In brief opening remarks, SRC Chairman Robert L. Archie Jr.

acknowledged recent "changes and challenges."

"Our main focus is the children," Archie said, "and going forward, we hope to pull the other distractions aside and focus on what is best for them and their future."

Ackerman, who has described herself as an educator done in by politics, did not attend the meeting, but many of her supporters were there.

State Rep. W. Curtis Thomas (D., Phila.) pointed out that earlier this year, the SRC extended Ackerman's contract through 2014, seemingly endorsing her performance.

"I can in no way support this proposed agreement," said Thomas, who praised Ackerman and her "Imagine 2014" strategic plan.

Activist Judith Robinson, who said Ackerman was treated with disrespect, took aim at the commission.

"Shame on this SRC," she said. "You've been derelict in your duties. Too much wheeling and dealing."

Speakers also demanded that the SRC release the names of those who made contributions used to buy out Ackerman. Those donations were funneled through the Philadelphia Children's First Fund, a nonprofit set up by the district and whose board once included Ackerman. Archie and acting Superintendent Leroy Nunery II are members.

"We want to know their intent and their motive," shouted Emmanuel Bussie, a frequent SRC critic. "Corporations don't do favors for nothing."

The government watchdog group Committee of Seventy has also formally asked the SRC to release the names of the donors.

"The inescapable message sent by this lack of transparency is that there is something to hide," committee president Zack Stalberg wrote in a letter to the SRC. "Moreover, keeping secret the names of donors prevents the public from knowing whether, or how, their favors might be returned."

Though most speakers supported Ackerman, even some who thought it was time for her to move on took the SRC to task.

"We need to regain control of our own school system," former district teacher Lisa Haver said. "I believe that this may not be the best model for our city. I believe a local Philadelphia school board would be better."

The SRC was created by a 2001 state-takeover law. Three members are appointed by the governor and two by the mayor.

Dressed all in white and carrying a large wooden staff, a speaker who identified herself as Mama Gail said, "It's no coincidence that the earth started to move the other day in New York and Philadelphia."

The Ackerman supporter warned of more trouble to come.

"Unless this is done right," she said, "there are going to be a whole lot more storms."

Vernard Johnson, an activist from Southwest Philadelphia, said, "What I liked about Dr. Ackerman is she stood up for black kids." Ackerman wasn't putting down other children, but was advocating for those most at risk, he said.

Williams also complained about Nunery's promotion.

"It just doesn't look right when somebody is lynched and her deputy winds up with her job," Williams said.

Earlier, Nunery introduced himself to the audience and said he was dedicated to the "ideals of education and advancement."

"With our 10th year of straight gains in achievement as a goal, we want to extend the legacy of Dr. Ackerman, but also keep intact the core mission of the School District of Philadelphia."

Nunery, who has worked at the University of Pennsylvania and the for-profit Edison Learning Inc., lacks a superintendent's certificate, but the SRC has the power to appoint him without one, and it did so Wednesday. He is paid $230,000.

The SRC declined to take questions after the meeting as school police officers physically barred reporters from approaching commission members.

State Auditor General Jack Wagner, who was prompted in part by the Ackerman deal to institute a new policy of auditing all superintendent contract buyouts, spoke out against the commission.

"I am appalled that the SRC is not listening to the public and their concerns," Wagner said. "The concerns are very basic: excessive salaries and confidential buyouts."

10 Tips on *Covering School Board and Goverment Meetings*

- Write the story in **third person**. No "**I.**"

- Set up your **computer or cell phone** to file on deadline.

- Read through the **agenda**. Put a check mark next to topics that look news worthy.

- Always write down: Actions taken; Who voted and how; How many people in the audience?

- **Stay till the very end**, even if it is late. That is when a lot of news occurs, after most of the crowd has gone home.

- Don't write the story chronologically. Determine the most **news-worthy item** and focus on that.

- Listen closely to the people who speak during **public comment**. Look on the sign up sheet for their name spellings or quickly go up to them afterwards.

- You will not understand everything that is going on. That's okay. **Talk** to government or school officials **after the meeting** and ask them questions.

- There will be lots of jargon and complicated acronyms discussed at the meeting. It is your job to explain things in **clear and concise language**.

- If you can, **don't sit with the other reporters**. You get a better sense of what's going on by sitting in the audience.

In-Class Activity/Homework

Find the website for the City Council or other governing body in your town, city or state.

WHEN and WHERE do they meet? _ _ _ _ _ _ _ _ _ _ _ _ _ _ _ _ _ _

WHO is the mayor? _

LOOK on the website for the names of the council members or school board members. WHO are they?

_ _

WHICH of these topics should be the main focus on the school board meeting story? WHY?

- The fifth graders of Central School read 100 books in 100 days.
- The school district needs to raise taxes by 10 percent in order to build a new high school.
- The superintendent, who is married, was caught having sex with his secretary in his office during school hours.

WHICH of these topics should be the main focus of a government story? WHY?

- The mayor fired the police chief because the crime rate increased 25 percent in two years.
- The Shade Tree Committee wants to buy a maple tree for outside Town Hall.
- Fifty residents showed up to complain about inadequate snow removal on their streets during the last blizzard.

Journalist Q&A

Courtesy of Garrick Goh

Kristen Graham

Where did you work?
The Philadelphia Inquirer.

What was your beat or job title?
Title, staff writer. I cover the Philadelphia School District, the nation's eighth-largest education system.

Where did you go to college? What was your degree?
Temple University, journalism degree.

Did you work on your college newspaper or online news website?
Yes! I was news editor of the Temple News, but also did a ton of freelancing for various publications when I was in college.

Did you have any internships? If so, where and what did you do?
Yes! I worked for two summers at the Inquirer. I was a general assignment reporter in the South Jersey bureau who wrote obituaries two days a week. My second summer, I covered three towns in suburban Philadelphia – hanging out at zoning boards, school boards, and town councils.

When and where was your first journalism job? What is one thing you learned from it?
I was hired by the Inquirer when I graduated from college in 2000. I worked in the South Jersey bureau covering local towns. One thing I learned from it is that no story is beneath you. That meeting may seem really boring and a waste of time, but you never know who you'll meet, or how that feature on the marching band will influence someone who could be a source for a much larger story.

What was the hardest part of your first journalism job?
The pay and the hours. I lived at home with my parents so I was able to maintain my three-meals-a-day habit, but it was a lean first couple of years. And I had to bid farewell to any semblance of a social life, because I was in night meetings almost every night, and often worked on the weekend.

Many beginning journalists get very nervous about their first assignments. Did you get nervous and how did you cope?

Yes! I've been a journalist for over a decade and I still get nervous before big assignments. I cope by arming myself with as many facts as possible about what I was writing about. Know your subject matter, and it will help to be calm! If you think you're going to blank out, write down a long list of questions in advance.

What is the worst part about being a journalist?

Two things: first, the hours. Still! The pay got better (somewhat) but the hours are still a real bear. Second, the uncertainty. The industry is changing in every conceivable way, and it feels like job security is out the window.

What is the best part?

Making a difference. Being able to help people by spreading information. Being able to right wrongs with what I write. Getting to learn about a million different things and meet people I'd never know otherwise. It's a tough job, but it's the most fun, fulfilling work I can think of.

What advice would you give to a journalism major?

Write! Get clips from every place you can think of – school paper, community papers, and online news outlets. And diversify your skill set. Learn to shoot video and photos. Be fluent in every kind of social media. Don't neglect the core skills of the trade – reporting and writing – but that's not enough any more.

What would you tell yourself at the beginning of your career, if you could go back in time?

Pack a sandwich. I can't count the number of times I've eaten crap because a story broke and I didn't have food with me. Don't check your e-mail on vacation – my husband especially has had to put up with an awful lot because of my job, and though it's tempting to be on duty 24/7, it's important to set boundaries.

Chapter 3
Police Reporting

Courtesy of David J. Gard

The police beat is one of the best and worst for a reporter. Stories from the beat are inherently dramatic – a kidnapped child; a murderer who killed in cold blood; a stupid criminal who robbed a bank with a note written on his own deposit slip. Cop stories are funny, pathetic, frightening, horrifying, disturbing, intriguing and absorbing. For a reporter with a literary soul, stories from this beat are some of the best out there and many get great play in the newspaper. Some of the best reporters are police reporters and some of the best novelists and non-fiction writers started out on the beat, too.

These stories are necessary. Citizens need to know who and where the "bad guys" are. They need to know when good cops turn bad and they need to pay attention when justice is not served.

In reporter terms, this is known as covering the "cops" beat, even though it encompasses much more than, well, cops. It is the repository of accidents, beatings, murders, fires, floods and malfeasance. Sources can include police officers, state troopers, sheriff's deputies, fire fighters, prosecutors and defense lawyers. Bad weather stories often fall under the cops beat, too.

Writing about cops and weather is typically the most labor-intensive for often the least payoff. Some of the cops beat is exciting – triple murder cases and escaped convicts. The rest is standing on the street watching a house burn in the freezing cold or making 50 phone calls to various clerks to try and get the correct age for an accident victim.

But there is always that one story, full of detail and drama that makes it all worthwhile.

One tip to keep in mind: Police stories are often covered by many reporters at the same time. Try to go off on your own, if you can, and avoid being stuck in pack coverage. Your story, photo or video will be better for it.

Here are some stories a reporter might cover on the police beat:

- Murders

- Rape

- Robberies

- Accidents

- Fires

- Natural Disasters

- Law enforcement news (new police chief or sheriff)

- Crime trends (certain items being stolen, such as copper pipes for quick cash)

There are two kinds of crime – felony and misdemeanor. Here are some examples of each:

FELONY: murder, manslaughter, rape, robbery, aggravated assault, kidnapping, grand theft auto, possession of drugs with intent to sell, hate crimes, terroristic threats, DUI with bodily harm or death

MISDEMEANOR: DUI, possession of marijuana under 1 gram, shoplifting, larceny, public intoxication, driving with a suspended license

The main difference between felonies and misdemeanors is the **severity** and **punishment**.

Felonies are more serious and carry a greater possibility of punishment – including state prison. Misdemeanors are less serious and if sentenced to jail, the person usually goes to county jail.

So where does a reporter get stories on the cops beat? There are several places, including:

- Police **scanner**

- Police **station**

- **Press releases**

- **Tips** from readers or viewers

- **Booking blotter** at the jail

- Information from **emergency dispatchers**

Reporter Cori Egan got thrust into a national story when she heard emergency calls over the police scanner one night in the newsroom of The Paducah Sun in Kentucky. Egan graduated from Rowan University and on the strength of her classes and internship experiences got her first job as a reporter in Paducah. It was during her second month at the job, during a bad storm, that she heard the emergency call about rescuers heading to a creek.

There comes a point, when you work breaking news and especially when you work the night shift, where you just mentally check out. When deadline is 11 p.m., that check out time is usually about 9:30 p.m. Inevitably, at least once a week, a call will come over the police scanner that clues you in to an accident or a fire that you have to rush out to.

That Thursday night in February, a call came over the scanner sending rescuers to a nearby county. Kentucky had had snow and rain for several days before that, and a rash of harsh storms that night had forced roads to be closed and flash flood warnings. I had spent most of my time that night running after water rescues and compiling accident briefs into one extremely long story on the storm.

The call that asked rescuers in our county to head over to Graves County wasn't like the others. They said children were missing. After checking all of the social media networks of our competitors, I had what I thought was the story: Two children were missing after playing in a creek.

I called my boss and got the OK to make the hour-long trip. I went down there with a photographer, amid storms that were producing nickel-sized hail and funnel clouds. By the time we got down there, it was clear that this wasn't a search for just two children.

Anyone within 50 miles was at "search headquarters," a Baptist church about a tenth of a mile from a creek. There were rescue crews from 30 different agencies set up in the parking lots. Community members of were making warm coffee. We got the full story from the sheriff a few minutes later. An Amish couple and their seven children had been on their way home that night when they got caught in the storm. Their buggy was swept away in the flood. The couple saved three of their children. The other four were missing.

I was on scene with the rescuers for close to an hour before my editor-in-chief came down there. We were careful not to interrupt the search, and called in to add to the story every 10 minutes or so. As details came in, I emailed our newsroom from my phone so page design workers could add to my story. We moved back the deadline a half-hour at a time, even delaying production twice.

Three of the four children were found just before midnight. They were close to each other, washed up on shore in an almost raging creek. They were dead. Before the sheriff told us anything, I saw one of the ambulances open its back doors and I watched as a crew hurried in. One moved just enough for me to see two little, black shoes.

The sheriff brought us into a back room shortly before midnight. It was just me and a television cameraman. He was visibly upset — in Kentucky, sheriffs are like fathers to their communities, everyone knows them and respects them and follows their rules. He told us, with a noticeable crack in his voice, that they had found three of the children. The search would continue for the fourth through the night and into the morning.

No matter how cluttered your thought process is, you have to just keep working. There are no mistakes allowed in breaking news. Because the incident had happened well after the 10 p.m. news, I was the only news outlet there that would have the story for people when they woke up. So even when I found out the children were as young as 5 months old, I couldn't cry. I couldn't be overwhelmed. I wrote. We used cell phone pictures as the dominant art.

On the long drive home in my editor's car, we checked several news sites. The TV station that always beat us out didn't have the updated story. The AP had picked up my story, edited it down, and versions were appearing on CNN and MSNBC, as well as other websites. It was a victory for newspapers, and one that I was proud to be part of.

That didn't allow me to escape the sadness. When I finally got into bed, there were no words to describe how upset I was. One of my colleagues did the follow-up the next day, and knowing the details sent me through a throng of emotions. They found the fourth child the next afternoon; our photographer was there to capture the aftermath.

He also shot one picture that shook me — a black bonnet, covered in mud and leaves — sitting along the creek bed. It was Elizabeth Yoder's, the 11-year-old who was the last to be recovered. I keep that picture in a file folder on my desktop to remind me how quickly life can change.

One of the toughest aspects of covering the cops beat is talking to grieving and upset family members and friends.

Don't expect it to be easy. But don't be surprised at how often people DO want to talk. Often, they work through their anger and grief by telling the story. But if the person does not want to talk, don't push it. At least not that day.

Never, never ask: "How do you feel?" No, just no. They will tell you how they feel. Really.

When talking to anyone even tangentially connected to a murder victim or other recently dead person you're writing about, precede your question with your condolences. It is not cloying; it shows you are human.

Most reporters on the Metro staff have to work the cops shift on certain weekends. That was my duty one summer day when I was working at the Palm Beach Post.

We got word that a young man had died of a drug overdose. The police department sent us some information that mentioned that the 20-year-old had ingested the powerful narcotic oxycodone, among other drugs, before dying. At that time, there were a number of young people dying from oxycodone overdoses because they would crush the time-release pills and snort them.

I drove to the home of the young man who had died, Vincent Bucciarelli, to try and talk to his family. No matter how many times I have had to interview family members after a death, it is never easy. I had a familiar queasy feeling in my stomach while I walked to the door and knocked.

A family friend answered the door and told me that Vincent's mother was inside, but she was upset and was resting. I tried to be calm, polite and sympathetic. The family friend sat with me on the front step for a while and we talked. He didn't want to be quoted. After a time, he went inside and asked Vincent's mother, Teresa, if she wanted to talk to me about her son.

Reluctantly, she did. Teresa Bucciarelli eventually let me inside her house and showed me photos of her youngest son. While we talked, I learned that she had gone to court to get her son committed to a drug rehabilitation facility. But the publicly funded rehab centers were all full and so her son died while he was on the waiting list.

Here's an excerpt from the story:

Drug law questioned as patients die in wait
The Palm Beach Post

Sept. 23, 2001

Kathryn Quigley, Staff Writer

WEST PALM BEACH — Late at night, Vincent Bucciarelli sobbed himself to sleep.

His mother, Teresa, heard the cries of her youngest son – her baby, even at 20. His anguish broke her heart.

In the mornings, he told her: "I hate these drugs, Mom. I don't want to do them, but I know I will."

Teresa Bucciarelli tried to help her son by using the courts to get him committed to drug treatment. But a lengthy waiting list at a local treatment center stymied her efforts.

While waiting for a bed, her son died Aug. 4 of a suspected drug overdose.

He is one of at least three substance abusers who died in the past year while waiting to get into one of the county's two treatment centers for people without money or insurance to cover the cost.

The problem, according to court officials familiar with the process: There simply are not enough drug treatment beds in the county for people who rely on the state to pay. The typical wait for one of the beds is four to eight weeks.

But there is another way for these people to get into treatment almost immediately: by getting arrested. The Department of Corrections pays for more treatment beds in Palm Beach County than does the Department of Children and Families, the agency that covers treatment for people who can't afford it.

"In order to get this treatment, your ticket is to commit a crime," said Judge Edward Rodgers, a retired Palm Beach County circuit judge who presides over commitment hearings at a special drug court in Riviera Beach.

Reporters should always carry the following items in their cars or backpacks:

- Raincoat. A poncho type is good because you can put your notebook underneath it and write without your notebook getting soaked.
- Change of clothes, including jeans, socks and shoes in case you have to tramp through the woods or stand in the middle of a highway in August.
- Water and some granola bars or other snacks. You never know when you're going to be stuck at a crime scene for hours.
- Bug spray and sunscreen.
- Extra notebooks and pens.
- Pencils, because pens don't write on wet paper in the rain.
- Phone numbers for all your police contacts on a piece of paper or in your phone.
- A good, up-to-date map, a map app or GPS.
- Boots.
- A hat.

10 Tips on *Covering the Police Beat*

- Many law enforcement officials are **suspicious** of the media. Don't be surprised if they act hostile to you at first.

- When calling police and fire dispatchers, don't just ask: "Is anything going on?" Be specific. "Are there any murders, rapes, robberies or fires tonight?

- When a story breaks, **just go**. Don't wait. Get up and go. (And stop at the bathroom on your way out the door.)

- **Double-check details**, like names and addresses. Cops are not Pulitzer-prize winning reporters. They can make mistakes.

- Don't follow the media horde. Get the information you need, then **go your own way**. Don't become part of the pack.

- **Don't convict the person in print**. Write that the person was "charged with murder" and not "arrested for murder." Innocent till proven guilty really is a true concept.

- Law enforcement officers tend to speak in jargon and catch phrases like "fled on foot." It is your job to **write in plain English**.

- **Attribute**. It covers your butt. Who said it?

- The stories might get to you. Be aware of that. **Be good to yourself**. It is okay to cry occasionally after the story is filed.

- People lie. Especially criminals.

In-Class Activity/Homework

Here is a press release from the New Jersey State Police. It is full of information and jargon. Turn this press release into a 300-400 word story, which is clear, concise and accurate. Remember to attribute the press release as your source.

NEW JERSEY STATE POLICE
OFFICIAL NEWS RELEASE
FOR FURTHER INFORMATION CONTACT:
Office of Public Information (609) 882-2000

FOR IMMEDIATE RELEASE:
June 23, 2011
Operation Fourth Down
Tackles Violent Bloods Set in Paterson

Totowa, NJ – Today at the State Police Troop B Headquarters in Totowa, Attorney General Paula T. Dow, Passaic County Prosecutor Camelia M. Valdes and New Jersey State Police Acting Deputy Superintendent of Investigations Major Matthew Wilson announced the stunning results of a nearly yearlong cooperative investigation into the drug distribution activities of a Paterson street gang. Arrests totaled more than 170 people, 29 of whom were taken into custody during early morning sweeps today in Paterson.

Those arrested included members of the Fruit Town Brims, a set of the Bloods street gang that operated out of the Fourth Ward of Paterson City. A large, multi-agency task force spread across the city early this morning to execute 9 search warrants and 24 arrest warrants. So far, 22 of the 24 sought on warrants were captured. In addition to the arrests, detectives prior to today have seized 12 guns, and more than 4,000 bags of heroin, crack, marijuana and other drugs. More drugs and cash were confiscated this morning.

Residents and elected officials in the city had raised concerns over drug distribution and violence in the streets of the Fourth Ward. The New Jersey State Police Street Gang Unit worked in conjunction with

33

the Regional Operations Intelligence Center's analysts to identify the Fruit Town Brims as the primary drug distribution network in the area. Troopers partnering with the Passaic County Prosecutor's Office, Passaic County Sheriff's Department, and the Paterson Police Department arrested drug dealers and buyers, and developed a picture of the gang hierarchy.

Detectives identified Tahir Canady, 25 of Paterson, Alshaquen Nero, 25 of Paterson, and Shabli Williams, 29 of Paterson, as members of the Fruit Town Brims and leaders of the narcotics distribution network. All three men were arrested on warrants this morning. Canady and Nero were charged with being the Leader of a Narcotics Trafficking Network, and other drug and weapons charges. Williams was charged with Leader of Narcotics Trafficking Network and related charges. All three will be lodged in the Passaic County Jail on $250,000.00 bail.

On two occasions during the investigation, detectives on surveillance observed men fire weapons at unknown subjects. On both occasions the subjects were arrested and the weapons were recovered. Tyrell Floyd, 19 of Paterson, and Asmar Williams, 19 of Paterson, were both charged with Unlawful Possession of a Weapon and related charges.

"Once again, through multi-agency partnerships, intelligence sharing and strategic targeting, New Jersey's law enforcement delivered a blow to the criminal gangs and drug dealers that have been creating havoc in our cities," said Attorney General Dow. "The arrests we have made during this targeted operation sends a message to the individuals who are bringing drugs and guns into our communities. This conduct will receive swift and certain consequences."

"The City of Paterson is safer today because of the hard work and dedication of the multiple law enforcement agencies involved in this 11-month investigation," said Prosecutor Valdes. "From the onset, this investigation was designed to identify, arrest and prosecute individuals and gangs responsible for violent crime and narcotics trafficking in Paterson. We are confident this large number of arrests will have a significant impact on reducing crime in our city today, and in the future."

"The people targeted in Operation Fourth Down were identified as prime movers in Paterson crime and drug distribution," said Major Matthew Wilson, Deputy Superintendent of the New Jersey State Police. "By identifying them through intelligence-led policing, and taking them out of play through cooperative law enforcement efforts, we have made a very real difference in the quality of life for the citizens in this area."

In order to get a view of the overall crime patterns of Paterson's fourth ward, State Police utilized the NJSP Regional Operations Intelligence Center (ROIC) P.O.P. Analysis Initiative. Under the authority of the New Jersey Attorney General's Office the NJ P.O.P. Initiative examines the criminal shooting environment in New Jersey and identifies significant problem areas, provides temporal and geo-spatial analysis, delineates gang related shootings, and draws associations between weapons recovered, recidivist offenders, and shooting motivations across jurisdictional boundaries. This initiative information is necessary for combating violent crime.

In addition to the NJ POP initiative, the New Jersey State Police is also an active partner in the Violent Enterprise Source Targeting (VEST) Program. The VEST program is an innovative, multi-agency collaborative effort to disrupt and dismantle violent criminal organizations in New Jersey. This program utilizes the resources of local, county, state and federal agencies to share intelligence, target the most violent offenders, conduct sustained enforcement operations, and coordinated prosecutions. During this investigation, the fourth ward was identified as a VEST target and one of the most violent areas in Paterson. Additional VEST partners, including the Passaic County Prosecutor's Office, Passaic County Sheriff's Department, Essex County Prosecutor's Office and the Paterson Police Department, assisted in this investigation.

. . . .

Use the space below to write your story.

Journalist Q&A

Eliot Kleinberg

Where do you work?
Palm Beach Post.

What is your beat or job title?
Staff writer, Southern Palm Beach County general assignment.

Where did you go to college and what was your degree?
B.S. news editing, University of Florida, 1977. B.S. broadcasting, University of Florida, 1978.

Did you work on your college's newspaper or online news website?
Yes.

Did you have any internships? If so, where and what did you do?
One semester, Gainesville Sun, 1977. General assignment.

When and where was your first journalism job? What is one thing you learned from it?
News producer/reporter, WNWS-AM news radio, 1979-1980. Should have learned to get out of broadcast news ASAP. Did learn how to produce on the fly. Learned importance of local news.

What was the hardest part of your first journalism job?
Working six days a week, starting 5 a.m. Working through drive time without having time to go potty.

Many beginning journalists get very nervous about their first assignments. Did you get nervous and how did you cope?
Terrified about getting a fact error. Still am.

What is the worst part about being a journalist?
Right now, that everyone believes you are incompetent and biased and a cog in a giant conspiracy, and yet simultaneously part of a dying industry.

What is the best part?

Telling people something they don't know. Every once in a while, moving someone. And yes, seeing your name in the paper.

What advice would you give to a beginning journalist?

As people turn more and more to the Internet, newspapers — and there may be a time we're not on paper, but whatever you want to call us — will become more and more critical. Already politicians have realized they can bypass a dogged and independent press and go directly to the people without being challenged. That's called propaganda and dictatorship. TV is too busy with car crashes, pet pictures and the winners of "Dancing with the Stars." Bloggers are about as responsible, and accountable, as the guy selling medicine in the alley. If Americans stopped for a second to realize the press is the only institution trying to find out the truth, and without it they are victims and sheep, they'd read more papers. I believe they're starting to catch on so I believe reports of our industry's death are greatly exaggerated.

What would you tell yourself at the beginning of your career, if you could go back in time?

Skip broadcasting and go right to papers. Instead of watching baseball at night, get going on your books.

Chapter 4
Covering Courts

Courtesy of Mark Torres

Forget everything you think you know about courts from watching movies or "Law and Order." Real life is nothing like television, especially since there is no "Gung! Gung!" sound in the background between every court hearing.

Covering courts can be tedious, depressing and overwhelming. You are writing about people at their worst possible moments – when they are forced to relive the day their father was murdered or the day their son was sentenced to prison for life.

Most lawyers and judges aren't glamorous and very few defendants are. The cases are petty, miserable and sad. The language is arcane, with phrases like *writ of certiorari* and *habeas corpus*. Depending on where you live, the sheer volume of court cases can be alarming.

But court cases can also be among the best stories to cover. At their heart, court cases are about the basic motivations of humans: love, greed, jealousy, anger and stupidity. The cases reek of tragedy, failed chances and idiocy. A 13-year-old throws his life away the day he brings a gun to school and kills his teacher. A young woman is murdered after she accepts a ride home from the wrong person. A child dies in the crossfire of a dumb dispute over drugs.

Court stories work so well because they include the three "Cs" of reporting: **color**, **conflict** and **characters**. The **color** is in the dialogue during the hearings and trials, and the details of the cases. The **conflict** is inherent: someone broke the law, someone is suing or someone's children have been taken away by the state.

The **characters** are the lawyers, judges, defendants, witnesses, jurors and family members who fill the courtrooms. All can be worth a story.

Many court reporters work directly with the police reporters at their publications or news organizations. The police reporters catch the stories when they first occur. The courts reporters follow the long, circuitous and often-tortured route through the legal system.

At first glance, covering courts can seem daunting. There is so much to do and so much to learn. But once you break it down, it is manageable.

First of all, there are two judicial systems: **federal** and **state**.

Federal court involves crimes which are prosecuted by the federal government, such as corruption or a nationwide child pornography ring. These cases are prosecuted by U.S. attorneys and presided over by federal judges.

The **state court** system is located in individual states, with local laws pertaining. There are lots of lower-level courts in the state system, such as municipal court or district court. These cases are prosecuted by state attorneys or district attorneys and by local judges.

Each of the court systems deals with two kinds of law: **criminal** and **civil**. A **criminal** case is when a law is broken that affects the general public, like a murder. These cases are sub-divided into serious crimes called **felonies** (such as murder) and lesser crimes called **misdemeanors** (such as public intoxication).

A **civil** case is when person or group sues another in a dispute over property, damages or breach of contract. Divorce, auto negligence and medical malpractice are all examples of civil court cases.

Juvenile court is both criminal and civil. For instance, a 10-year-old charged with throwing a brick from an overpass onto the highway would be heard in the delinquency side of juvenile court. But the case of a 10-year-old removed from his home after being abused by his parents would be handled in the dependency side of juvenile court. Laws vary from state to state for covering juvenile court, but it is a gold mine of stories about children in trouble with the law and children in need of help. Often, they are the same children.

One of the saddest stories I covered was in 2001 when I was part of the reporting team of the Palm Beach Post at the trial of Nathaniel Brazill, a 13-year-old who killed his seventh-grade teacher with a handgun on the last day of school in May 2000.

Prosecutors in Florida offered Nathaniel a plea deal of 25 years in prison. His mother, Polly Powell, turned it down and Nathaniel was convicted and sentenced to 28 years in prison.

This story involved **color** – the state was trying a 13-year-old for murder in adult court. Most of the people involved, from Nathaniel himself to his classmates who testified as witnesses, were good examples of **characters**. And the **conflict** could not have been more apparent – the state said Nathaniel killed his teacher, Barry Grunow, in a premeditated way. He said the gun went off by accident.

I was in the courtroom covering the case on April 26, 2001 when his mother rejected the plea deal. The judge wanted to make sure Nathaniel and his mother knew exactly what they were doing, so he asked them, over and over.

Judge Confronts Brazill, Parents on Rejected Plea Deal

The Palm Beach Post

April 26, 2001

Kathryn Quigley, Staff Writer

WEST PALM BEACH — Circuit Judge Richard Wennet leaned toward the microphone and swiftly changed the direction of Thursday's pretrial hearing for 14-year-old murder defendant Nathaniel Brazill.

"I want to explore the plea rejection with the defendant and his family," Wennet said sharply after preliminary jury selection ended.

Last week, Brazill and his family rejected an offer that called for 25 years in prison in exchange for a guilty plea to second-degree murder.

"You understand that, while you're just 14 years old, this decision you've made, you may have to live with for the rest of your life?" Wennet asked Brazill.

"Yes, sir," Brazill said quietly.

Brazill is charged with the first-degree murder of teacher Barry Grunow at Lake Worth Middle School May 26. If convicted of the charge, Brazill would go to prison for life.

Also Thursday, Wennet and lawyers for both sides chose 18 more people who said they could judge Brazill fairly. Those prospective jurors and 44 chosen the day before will return Monday for more intense questioning as the lawyers whittle the pool to 12 jurors, plus two alternates. Opening arguments may begin Tuesday.

When the last of the jury pool was sent home, Wennet asked Brazill's parents, Polly Powell and Nathaniel Brazill Sr., to move to the front of the courtroom. He asked for the undivided attention of Brazill, his lawyers and prosecutors. Grunow's relatives also stayed in the room.

Several times and in several ways, Wennet asked the teen and his parents whether they understood the ramifications of going to trial: a possible life sentence.

Each time the answer was the same.

"Yes, sir," Brazill said.

After the hearing, Brazill's parents, who are divorced, said they have faith the jurors would find in their son's favor. Twenty-five years in prison was just too much for a 14-year-old, Powell said.

"I wasn't going to accept that at all," she said.

In a recent Fort Lauderdale case that also gained national attention, the mother of 14-year-old Lionel Tate turned down an offer of three years in juvenile detention and 10 years' probation. Instead, he was sentenced to life in prison after a jury found him guilty of first-degree murder for beating his 6-year-old playmate to death.

Assistant State Attorney Marc Shiner won't comment on the Brazill case before it's over.

Prosecutors probably will argue at trial that Brazill was angry after being suspended from school earlier in the day. According to investigators, he went home, got a gun, brought it to school and shot Grunow hours after telling another student he was going to be "all over the news."

Brazill's lawyer, Robert Udell, even told would-be jurors Thursday that Brazill shot Grunow.

"I can tell you right now, we concede he did it, but he still might not necessarily be guilty of murder," Udell said.

Udell said Brazill wants to tell jurors during the trial that the gun went off accidentally and he didn't mean to hurt Grunow.

"Nate has a lot of faith in the criminal justice system," Udell said after the hearing. "He believes the truth will come out."

Besides first-degree murder, the jury could be asked to decide whether Brazill is guilty of lesser charges — second-degree murder or manslaughter — or not guilty at all. Brazill also is charged with aggravated assault with a firearm for pointing the gun at another teacher.

Wennet scheduled preliminary jury selection because of intense pre-trial publicity. He called 180 people into court over two days and dismissed 118 who said they could not judge Brazill fairly or devote two weeks to the case.

Today, the lawyers will discuss a prosecutors' request for a psychiatrist to examine Brazill.

Covering courts is not all sadness and strife. Court cases, especially civil courts, can be a window to how the "other half" lives.

Here are the top three paragraphs of a story I wrote about the arrest of a matchmaker who charged up to $25,000 per client. The story ran in the Palm Beach Post on June 13, 2002:

Boca Matchmaker Awaits Her Date – With a Judge

The Palm Beach Post

June 13, 2002

Kathryn Quigley, Staff Writer

BOCA RATON – The cops collared Cupid Wednesday, arresting an international matchmaker accused of breaking dozens of lonely hearts and defrauding them of millions.

For $5,000 and much more, Helena Amram promised perfect partners for clients shopping for soulmates at her dating salons in New York, Tel Aviv, Beverly Hills and Boca Raton.

At best, her dates were losers, more than a few complained. Other grateful customers said she did deliver Prince or Princess Charming.

But not too many, according to authorities. After a six-month investigation, Boca Raton police decided that what Amram did to her dissatisfied customers was a crime. They charged Amram, 52, with defrauding 54 clients out of more than $2.7 million.

Also arrested Wednesday was her 55-year-old husband, Itamar, listed as the owner of Soulmate by Helena, 2424 N. Federal Highway. They set up shop here in 1998 and lived in Mizner Park.

Attorney Michael B. Cohen said Helena Amram is a sick woman whose condition has been made worse by unfounded allegations. She suffers from lupus and epilepsy, he said, and spent time in a hospital's intensive care unit last month.

"She vigorously denies the validity of these charges," Cohen said. "She's very sick as a result of the stress."

The couple was released from the Palm Beach County Jail after each posted $15,000 bond.

Amram has jet-black hair, an exotic accent and three Social Security numbers. In an array of publications, including the Wall Street Journal and The New York Times, she boasted of marrying off thousands of couples. Even celebrity news anchor Connie Chung did a piece about her in 1990.

Boca police say Amram left dozens of singles in Palm Beach, Broward and Miami-Dade counties with nothing more than worthless handwriting analyses and dates from hell.

Some clients said they paid $25,000 for dates who Amram claimed had been thoroughly screened for criminal pasts as well as for medical and psychological problems. In reality, police say, Amram faked some reports.

Police said she took money from many men and women but delivered no dates. When they complained, she allegedly told them they were "too fat" for her to find anyone interested.

Her brochure described "The Helena Concept," which claimed that only the "most desirable people" were accepted as clients. But former employees told police that Amram would lie. Instead of using fees to find dream dates, police said, she paid off her own credit card bills and took trips.

Boca Raton police Detective Robert Flechaus cracked the case by tracking down Amram's clients all over the country. He said the Amrams were "cooperative" when they surrendered to police Wednesday morning. The Amrams knew they were under investigation after police served a search warrant on their office in February - and hauled away computers and filing cabinets.

Amram's arrest brings her globe-trotting career to a dead stop, at least for now. She left New York in 1991 with numerous civil lawsuits unanswered and an unpaid judgment of $5.6 million. She moved to Beverly Hills, Calif., in 1992 to run a matchmaker business, but left in 1995 as the Beverly Hills police were about to file grand theft and deceptive advertising charges against her, according to her Boca Raton arrest report.

In 1997, she was running her business in Tel Aviv and living in a luxurious penthouse. She moved to Boca Raton a year later.

Three civil lawsuits have been filed against her in Palm Beach County, including one from 40-year-old Randie Kaiser of Miami-Dade. Kaiser sued the matchmaking company after she paid $20,000 after Helena Amram held her hands and told her she could "see into her soul" to help her find a man.

In her lawsuit, Kaiser said she went out on three dates who were completely unsuitable. When she complained, Helena Amram showed Kaiser pictures of pretty women. Stop being so picky, Amram allegedly told her. "This is your competition."

Amram's arrest showed Kaiser was right to feel cheated, said her attorney, J. Ronald Denman.

"Hopefully the truth will now come out," he said, "and this will prevent others from having to go through what Randie did."

Here are some terms that a reporter covering courts needs to know:

- Judge – the person who presides over the court. He/she may be a city, state or federal judge

- Bailiff – a legal officer in charge of the court; often a sheriff's deputy

- District Attorney/State Attorney – the office of the Prosecutor (the name varies by state)

- Plaintiff/Petitioner – the person or entity filing the court action

- Defendant/Respondent – the person or entity being charged or sued

- Indictment – a formal accusation of a crime

- Arraignment – in a criminal case, when the defendant is informed of the charges and his/her right to an attorney

- Preliminary hearing – evidence is presented by both sides and a judge decides whether or not the case may proceed, or if the charges/lawsuit will be dismissed

- Appeal – after a conviction or sentence, the person or entity can ask a higher court to look at the case again; overturn the verdict/sentence or dismiss the verdict/sentence

In another court case, I wrote about the lawsuit filed against real estate magnate Donald Trump by his former chef, who sued for age discrimination. The lawsuit was filed after the chef was told "You're fired!" Here is the story:

Fired Mar-a-Lago Chef Claims Age Discrimination
The Palm Beach Post
January 22, 2002
Kathryn Quigley, Staff Writer

WEST PALM BEACH - Was the sauce too rich? Were the truffles too chewy?

Is that why Bernard Goupy was fired as the executive chef at Mar-a-Lago?

Or was Goupy canned because, at age 62, he was too stale for the ritzy denizens of Donald Trump's resort?

The French chef has filed an age discrimination lawsuit in Palm

Beach County Circuit Court and is seeking back pay and damages.

Trump said he didn't fire Goupy because he was too old; he fired him because he was a bad chef.

Celine Dion and her husband, Rene Angelil, don't seem to think so. They hired Goupy a few months ago as their personal chef. In a way, they got Trump's leftovers. But in Goupy, they also got an award-winning chef who has worked in high-priced hotels and restaurants all over the world.

Goupy now cooks for the songstress and her family at their home in Jupiter. He also travels with the couple and their baby boy, Rene-Charles.

Goupy's new famous bosses can't escape the long, wealthy and influential arm of Donald Trump, however. Dion and Angelil are scheduled to give videotaped depositions on Jan. 23 at the West Palm Beach office of Mar-a-Lago's lawyer, John Marion.

Marion was out of town and unavailable for comment about what he intends to ask Dion and Angelil.

Goupy's lawyer, William J. Berger, said Mar-a-Lago is trying to harass its former chef by dragging his current employers into his lawsuit.

"It would seem to me to be unnecessary to videotape Celine Dion and her husband at a deposition," Berger said. "It has to be annoying for them to be videotaped."

Goupy claims in court documents that when he was hired in August 2000, he was given a verbal promise by Bernd Lembcke, the managing director at Mar-a-Lago, that he would be paid $80,000 for a full year's employment. Instead, Goupy was fired six months later - and soon replaced by a younger chef in his 30s.

Goupy, of Delray Beach, is suing to get the remaining $40,000 he says Mar-A-Lago owes him.

Trump said he has no intention of paying Goupy any more money.

"He got fired because he was a terrible chef," Trump said on Thursday. "We didn't like his food."

Trump wouldn't be more specific.

"People didn't like it," he said. "I didn't like it."

Trump also denied the accusation of age discrimination.

"I hired him at the same age I fired him," Trump said.

Since Goupy's departure, guests at Mar-a-Lago tell Trump they like the food much better now, he said.

Mar-a-Lago is Trump's spectacular home in Palm Beach. Trump

bought the former Marjorie Merriweather Post home for $15 million in 1985 and turned the mansion into a private membership club. The resort hosts extravagant banquets, brunches, charity events and parties. Television talk show host Regis Philbin is expected to perform for Mar-a-Lago members and guests this weekend.

Goupy was trained to cook in his native France and has worked as an executive chef in elegant hotels around the world, including the Hilton chain in the Middle East and Wyndham hotels in the Caribbean. In the United States, he worked at such swank places at Chateau Elan in Georgia.

In 1993, he was named a Master Chef of France – a prestigious designation given only to chefs who maintain a high quality of professionalism and experience.

That doesn't figure into Mar-a-Lago's assessment of Goupy's skills, however. Court documents from Mar-a-Lago state that Goupy was fired because of complaints about: the quality of the food; the menu choices; the menu changes and his inability to manage the financial aspect of his position.

In other words, they didn't like him as a head chef.

Goupy's lawyer said it's all untrue.

"He was a good chef and he got along with people," Berger said.

Goupy's job as executive chef at Mar-a-Lago involved more administrative work - such as planning menus and hiring staff - than actual food preparation, Berger said. He helped run banquets and dinners more often than making actual meals, the lawyer said.

He may have a new job, but Goupy still wants to fight over his old one. While the case winds its way through the court system, Goupy's cooking will go on and on.

Now, it's just in Celine Dion's kitchen.

Covering courts involves walking up and down a lot of hallways, peeking into a lot of courtrooms and checking a lot of dockets. The process can feel tedious at times. If you forget to check just one day that is the day when an accused murderer makes an unexpected guilty plea and your competition gets the scoop.

You don't want that to happen.

Most courts reporters settle into a routine. For instance, they go to the courthouse early in the morning, around 8:30 a.m. or 9 a.m., to stop into court hearings and chat with lawyers. Many story ideas come from lawyers who are standing in the halls between court hearings, or in the snack bar getting coffee.

Become friendly with the security guards at the courthouse entrance, the court clerks, judges' secretaries and the bailiffs. They know when something important is happening in a case. An important thing to know is that there is no sign above a courtroom reading: "Great Story in Here Today." You have to show up, listen and find the story.

The next thing a courts reporter should do is check the docket. That is the list of court cases being heard that day. In some courthouses, the docket is available online. In others, it is bound in a book in the clerk's office. Some dockets are posted on the doors of the courtrooms. Others are guarded jealously by court clerks who want to know why a reporter wants to look at the docket.

Don't worry. The docket is public record and you don't have to explain why or who you are looking for. In criminal court, it lists the charges, the person charged, the courtroom number and the judge. In civil court it lists who is suing who, the courtroom and the judge. The names of the lawyers are usually listed as well.

And what you are looking for are serious crimes and well-known names. Most murder cases should give you pause, unless you live in a large city where the murders number into the hundreds and you simply can't cover them all.

Look for names of people charged with crimes or being sued. If the mayor is charged with soliciting prostitution, that is a story. If the mayor is charged with BEING a prostitute, that is an even bigger story.

In civil court, a reporter should look for cases involving a large sum of money, such as a medical malpractice suit in which the plaintiff is asking for $10 million. Civil cases are noteworthy if they involve people of prominence or if the facts are just plain odd, such as the famous case in which a woman sued after hot coffee spilled on her lap and scalded her.

The majority of civil court cases are dismissed or settled. But sometimes they go to trial. So do many criminal court cases, unless there is a plea bargain.

Here is the basic outline of a typical court trial:

- Jury selection (this is called *voir dire*). Criminal cases need 12 jurors.

- Opening statements – each side gets to present arguments and preview the evidence.

- Prosecution/Plaintiff's case – this side goes first, presenting witnesses and evidence.

- Cross examination – after each witness, the defense gets to question the witnesses.

- Rebuttal – the prosecutor or plaintiff's side gets to question their witnesses again.

- Defense case – now it's the other side's turn to present its case. (Cross examination from the prosecutor/plaintiff follows)

- Rebuttal – Defense gets to rebut the prosecution/plaintiff cross exam.

- Motions – after all the testimony, the defense might make a motion for the judge to dismiss the case.

- Closing arguments – both sides get a last chance to sum up their cases.

- Charge to the jury – the judge explains the law to the jury. In a criminal case, the jury must find guilt "beyond a reasonable doubt," but in a civil case, the burden of proof is lower – "a preponderance of evidence."

- Deliberations – the jurors elect a foreman and decide whether to convict or acquit (criminal case) or find liable or not liable (civil case).

- Verdict – what the jury decided.

- Sentence – if found guilty, the person could be sentenced to county jail, state or federal jail or probation and fines. In a civil case, there is no jail time. Instead, the jury finds fault (or not) and can assess damages to be paid.

10 Tips on *Covering the Courts Beat*

- **Be there.** To cover a courthouse, you must spend time there. Go every day, even if it's just for an hour. Go during peak times, such as morning hearings, when the most attorneys are walking the halls. Become a fixture. Get to the point where lawyers and courthouse workers notice when you're not at a hearing and they give you a call.

- Learn how the **courthouse works.** When time are status hearings? When can you look at the latest civil filings? When do particular judges typically issue their major orders — the beginning of the day or the end of the day? When is the best time to look up court files without having to wait in a long line?

- Learn the **courthouse docketing system**. Spend time getting to know the courthouse's computers, learning what information is available to you.

- Do your **homework**. Before covering a case, do the background work. Read the case file, read any articles you can get your hands on, read up on the attorneys involved.

- Don't just cover criminal court. Most news organizations typically focus on the criminal side of the courthouse. But there are great stories to be had in **civil, small claims and probate courts**.

- **Make friends** with court clerks, bailiffs and secretaries. They are the ones who know what is REALLY going on in the courthouse.

- **Juvenile court** can have a wealth of stories. Find out the law in your state about whether or not you can attend court hearings on juvenile crime and child welfare.

- **Courtroom benches** are hard. Bring a **cushion.**

- Courtrooms are usually too cold or too hot. **Dress in layers**.

- Turn **OFF your cell phone** or else face the wrath of the judge and probably get kicked out of the courtroom.

In-Class Activity/Homework

Some court cases are just plain goofy. One of the best websites to take a peek at weird and wacky legal documents is TheSmokingGun.com. The Smoking Gun uploads mug shots, police reports and court documents of the rich, famous and strange. Read the court document posted below about the man who was upset – VERY upset – that his Taco Bell order did not contain hot sauce. Read the charging document and then write a 400-word story on the case and the arrest.

STATE OF MISSOURI   )
) ss.
COUNTY OF JACKSON   )

AFFIDAVIT

I, Mark E. Corbin, being duly sworn, state and affirm the following:

1.   I am a Detective with the Lee's Summit, Missouri Police Department (LSPD) and have been so employed since April 4, 1998. I am currently assigned to the Federal Bureau of Investigation (FBI), Criminal Enterprise Squad to investigate gangs, drug violations and criminal enterprises within the Kansas City metropolitan area. Based upon the investigation, along with information provided to me by other law enforcement sources, I believe the following to be true and correct.

2.   On September 17, 2011, at approximately 11:28 p.m., the Lee's Summit, Missouri Police Department (LSPD) was dispatched on a 911 report of an armed disturbance at the Taco Bell, 615 NW Libby Lane, Lee's Summit, Jackson County, Missouri.

3.   Upon arrival, uniformed officers discovered the 911 call for service was in regards to a white male, driving a two-tone blue over silver Ford F-150 pointing a shotgun at Taco Bell drive-thru employee, Jacob R. McDonald.

4.   McDonald reported that the white male suspect drove next to the Taco Bell drive-thru window to complain that his (suspect's) order was wrong. McDonald stated the suspect handed the wrong order of food back to him (McDonald) through the drive-thru window and then reached for a shotgun, which had shells on the side, in the front passenger area of the Ford F-150. McDonald said once he (McDonald) saw the shotgun he (McDonald) turned to run from the drive-thru window. In addition to providing a suspect vehicle description, McDonald informed uniformed officers that the suspect was intoxicated, and had a goatee with a bandage around his (suspect's) left hand.

5.   On September 18, 2011, at approximately 1:15 a.m., uniformed officers of the LSPD located the possible suspect vehicle (based on color, make, model and items contained within the bed of the truck provided by the victim and surveillance video), a blue over silver Ford F-150 which displayed Missouri license plate 4MF652, in the driveway of 406 NW O'Brien Road, Lee's Summit, Jackson County, Missouri. Uniformed officers conducted a residence check at the aforementioned residence. Upon contacting homeowner, Vicki L. Squires, she (Squires) identified the owner of the Ford F-150 as her nephew, Jeremy W. Combs. While at the residence uniformed officers contacted Combs, and observed him (Combs) to be highly intoxicated, and having a splint on his (Combs') left pinkie finger, which included having tape wrapped around his (Combs') left hand. Combs denied leaving the residence on September 17, 2011, indicating that he (Combs) was home all day drinking beer.

6.   On September 18, 2011, at approximately 9:45 a.m., LSPD Sergeant John King and LSPD Detective Phillip Tucker responded to 406 NW O'Brien Road, Lee's Summit, Jackson County, Missouri, to conduct a follow-up investigation. Upon arrival, Combs contacted Sergeant King outside the residence near the Ford F-150 (4MF652, MO). Sergeant King inquired about Combs' willingness to allow officers conduct a search of the vehicle. Combs denied consent. Additionally, Sergeant King placed Combs under arrest for the armed assault, which occurred on September 17, 2011, at the Taco Bell, 615 NW Libby Lane, Lee's Summit, Jackson County, Missouri. Combs was transported to LSPD Headquarters for questioning. Additionally, LSPD Detectives prepared State of Missouri Circuit Court search warrants for: 406 NW O'Brien Road, Lee's Summit, Missouri; Ford F-150 and a BUCCAL swab from Combs.

7.   On September 18, 2011, at approximately 3:05 p.m., Sergeant King and Detective Tucker conducted an interview of Combs under *Miranda*, which was videotaped. During the interview, Combs admitted purchasing several food items from Taco Bell, 615 NW Libby Lane, Lee's Summit, Missouri, on September 17, 2011. Combs stated he (Combs) then drove to his (Combs') residence at 406 NW Libby Lane, Lee's Summit, Missouri. Upon arrival at home, Combs discovered the Taco Bell employee had failed to include his (Combs) hot sauce. Combs added he (Combs) became upset and drove back to the Taco Bell to confront the employee. Combs admitted to confronting the Taco Bell employee, but denied possessing a firearm. Sergeant King questioned Combs about the evidence captured via Taco Bell's surveillance camera. Combs responded that the item observed was a tire iron. Upon being questioned if the item was gun rather than a tire iron, Combs requested his attorney.

8.   On September 18, 2011, at approximately 8:30 p.m., LSPD detectives executed a signed State of Missouri Circuit Court search warrant at 406 NW O'Brien Road, Lee's Summit, Jackson County, Missouri. During the execution of the search warrant, detectives recovered a Mossberg, Model 500A, 12 gauge shotgun, (no serial number located), with five (5) live rounds of 12 gauge ammunition affixed to the side of the weapon under the bed mattress in Combs room. Additionally, detectives recovered clothing items similar to clothing worn by Combs, which was captured by the Taco Bell surveillance system.

9.   On September 18, 2011, LSPD detectives requested a criminal history records check on Combs. The resulting check revealed fourteen (14) felony arrests and three (3) felony convictions. Combs showed felony convictions for: Assault in the First Degree (guilty plea date of May 3, 1999) and Armed Criminal Action (guilty plea date of May 3, 1999).

10.   On September 19, 2011, at approximately 8:00 a.m., Combs re-contacted LSPD Detective Cox. Combs requested to speak with Detective Cox in regards to his (Combs') charges. Detective Cox again advised Combs of his (Combs') rights under *Miranda*. During the interview, Combs acknowledged possessing the firearm. Furthermore, Combs stated that he had purchased the firearm from "Mark" at a drug house in Independence, Missouri.

11.   On September 19, 2011, at approximately 12:12 p.m., I telephonically contacted Bureau of Alcohol, Tobacco, Firearms and Explosives (ATF) Special Agent (SA) Steve Lester in regards to the manufacturing location of the Mossberg 500A shotgun. SA Lester and ATF SA Gordon Mallory advised the Mossberg 500A shotgun was not manufactured in the State of Missouri and therefore, traveled in interstate commerce to reach the State of Missouri.

FURTHER AFFIANT SAYETH NAUGHT.

/s/ Mark E. Corbin
 MARK E. CORBIN
Task Force Officer
Federal Bureau of Investigation

Subscribed and sworn to before me

on this ___19th___ day of September, 2011.

/s/ John T. Maughmer
HONORABLE JOHN T. MAUGHMER
United States Magistrate Judge
Western District of Missouri

Use this space to write your story.

Journalist Q&A

Courtesy of Josh P. Miller

Kent German

Where do you work?
CNET.com

What is your beat or job title?
Senior Managing Editor, Mobile Reviews

Where did you go to college and what was your degree?
Univ. of San Francisco, BA
Communication

Did you work on your college newspaper or online news website?
Yes. One year as News Editor, one year as Editor-in-Chief

Did you have any internships? If so, where and what did you do?
Just one, a beat reporter at the Sierra Madre News in Sierra Madre, Calif.

When and where was your first journalism job? What is one thing you learned from it?
My first job after grad school was at Upside, a national tech and business magazine in San Francisco. I worked there for two years first as an assistant editor and then as an associate editor. The magazine closed in 2002. I learned the basics of developing content for an audience. I wasn't just writing stories that someone else assigned to me. I was planning it and making it happen for sections of a magazine.

What was the hardest part of your first journalism job?
The hardest part of the job was losing it when the magazine closed. But before then, the hardest part dealing with the tumultuous changes the magazine went through as the economy crashed. My first editor, who I really liked, was forced to resign. And in his place came someone who made a lot of bad decisions. Layoffs began and it was hard to keep focused and do my job.

Many beginning journalists get very nervous about their first assignments. Did you get nervous and how did you cope?

My first big story was on the proliferation of DSL Internet service and the challenges that providers faced in rolling out the technology. It was a long feature (a few thousand words) that took a lot of interviews. I wasn't really nervous, but it took a lot of research to make sure I was getting the technical terms correct.

What is the worst part about being a journalist?

Keeping a balance between your loyalty to your organization and telling the story and a loyalty to your sources (particularly when they're anonymous). You have to remember that what you write affects people and can have real consequences. And sometimes, people who have done nothing wrong can get hurt. You have to be able to divorce yourself from the emotion involved.

What is the best part?

The fact that every day is different. And the fact that you're uniquely involved in events shaping your community (however you want to define it).

What advice would you give to a journalism major?

Remember that your career may not always the track that you've laid out for yourself. By all means dream and go after what you want. Along the way, however, your career make unexpected detours that you didn't account for. When those happen, it doesn't mean your plans are changed. Rather, they might just be on hold for a while.

What would you tell yourself at the beginning of your career, if you could go back in time?

Be patient, don't take it all too seriously, and be nice to yourself.

Chapter 5
Natural Disasters and Bad Weather

Courtesy of Kevin Canessa

When it snows, school children get a day off. But for journalists, a huge snowstorm or any other kind of big weather story means a day on. When most people run from hurricanes, wildfires, blizzards, earthquakes and floods — journalists run toward the danger.

But that doesn't mean that journalists need to put themselves in danger. There is a smart way to cover natural disasters, so that journalists have the least chance of being in harm's way. For instance, one of the first rules for covering hurricanes is not to tether yourself to a building and then stand in the storm while the wind whips you around. But many television reporters will never listen to that advice.

This chapter is for everyone else, especially those journalists with an ounce of sense and a healthy respect for the dark side of Mother Nature.

There are many kinds of weather stories and natural disasters that turn into big news stories. Here are a few of them that you may encounter as a journalist.

Wildfires

In July 1998, much of the eastern part of Florida was on fire. A combination of a very wet weather, which let the underbrush grow out of control, and a very dry winter, which made the brush like tinder, caused a series of wildfires. The fires were so widespread that the flames could be seen from space.

Most reporters in Florida covered the wildfires that summer, dealing with smoke, heat and flames. Such fires happen often in Florida and in the western United States, especially California. Brush fires are part of the ecosystem and have the potential to cause millions of dollars in damage.

Fires are tricky – they create their own wind and can change direction at any second. A spot where a reporter was safe can turn deadly a minute later. They are deadly for residents, too. The entire population of Flagler County in Florida – more than 30,000 people – had to evacuate during the wildfires.

Reporters can feel overwhelmed during a wildfire occurrence, because there are so many fires and they happen so frequently. Cover the magnitude of the story, of course – how many acres burned, how many homes evacuated, injuries to residents and firefighters.

But focus on the people, too. In one story, I wrote about a newly-married man who had to evacuate quickly when the area around his Florida home caught fire in the summer of 1998. He grabbed only a few things – including his new wife's wedding gown. They had been married only 11 months and he knew the gown was important to her.

It was quite surreal to drive along a highway in Central Florida while trees burned right up to the road on either side. The fires were so widespread that the firefighters were letting some of the blazes burn out, instead of trying to put them all out. My hair and clothes smelled like smoke for weeks and the acrid scent lingered in the air.

Many reporters worked long hours in dirty conditions to get the story. We learned to be prepared and to be careful. But some people still take strange risks. For instance, one female reporter showed up for work wearing flip-flops. To cover a fire. She wore a skirt, too. Her rationale? It was going to be hot so she wanted her feet to feel cool. Huh.

When natural disasters occur, often journalists are wrung out once it's over. But there are still more stories to cover. Find a second wind and cover them.

After the Florida wildfires, I interviewed some local firefighters about their experiences. This is an excerpt from my story, which ran in the Orlando Sentinel on July 8, 1998:

Firefighter Mike Jacobs watched the firestorm roar toward him and thought about death. At that moment last week, in the woods near Mims as the trees turned from green to charred black in just seconds, Jacobs began to pray.

"Oh Lord, get me out of here and take care of my family if I don't," Jacobs recalled praying.

The Leesburg firefighter and his partner, Daryl Meeks, made it through the Brevard County firestorm by crouching low and staying calm.

The men were among 60 firefighters from Lake County, Mount Dora, Eustis and Tavares who assisted in fighting the brush fires that spread across the state in the past month.

The local firefighters traveled to Brevard, Volusia and Flagler counties to help control the blazes. Most of the firefighters worked long hours in extreme conditions, while others were used as standby help to relieve other tired firefighters.

The magnitude of the fires awed them, while the unpredictability of the blazes frustrated them. But they said the camaraderie of working with fellow firefighters from all over the country lifted their spirits, while the gratitude of the residents whose homes they saved made the effort worth it.

Tornadoes

Tornadoes kill hundreds of people every year, especially in middle part of the nation. They are so scary because they occur with limited warning and their path is always uncertain. Tornadoes can accompany hurricanes, can come in multiples or just appear by themselves.

Even if your part of the country doesn't usually experience tornadoes doesn't mean it won't in the future. Tornadoes can and do pop up in many places, including Northeastern cities. I once stood in front of a plate glass window in Philadelphia watching a tornado with a bunch of other people and we had no idea a tornado was passing by. We just thought it was windy. In retrospect, we should have been on the floor, covering our heads.

The best source for information is the National Weather Service (NWS), where you can get information about a tornado's projected path, its strength (the Enhanced F-scale) and its damage.

If a tornado is forecast, pay attention to whether it is a tornado **watch** or **warning**. According to the NWS, a **watch** means a tornado could form. A **warning** means one already did.

The worst place to be during a tornado is in a mobile home. If you are in one, get out. If you are driving, don't try to out-run the storm. Find a sturdy building and go inside. If you can't find a building, pull over, lie flat in a low spot and cover your head. Really. Forget about storm chasing, like in the movie "Twister," unless you want to get killed.

An annoying aspect of covering tornadoes is that nearly every person you interview afterwards will tell you that "it sounded like a train." This is because it does. But the comment is among the worst clichés in journalism. Try your best to get the person to explain the tornado WITHOUT using the train analogy.

In 1995, I covered a tornado that swept through two rural counties of North Carolina. One woman gave me the best quote I ever got about what it's like when a tornado whips by.

"It was like when you are in a really small car on the highway and an 18-wheeler passes by," she said.

See? That is a MUCH better description than "it sounded like a train."

Floods

New Jersey native **Rich Wisniewski** left his home to move all the way to Minot, ND when he got hired at NBC affiliate KMOT-TV. Wisniewski had been on the job only a few months when the station started reporting on a possible flood threat to the nearby Souris River. Most residents didn't take the threat too seriously, though, because the town had a levee system. But a severe winter with lots of heavy snow, plus a heavy rain storm in June 2011 caused the river to flood its banks. The flooding soon became a national story and Wisniewski was in the middle of it.

Where do you work and what is your beat?

I work in Minot, ND as a General Assignment Reporter. I work in a small market and I'm a small market reporter which means me and my three other reporters don't really have "one" beat. But when I got hired I was told I would be the health reporter. However, I also work closely with the police department in Minot and I also made contacts win Burlington, ND, which is a small town about a mile out of Minot. Note: The town of Burlington flooded a day before Minot, so while everyone was getting set for Minot's flood, I was off in Burlington keeping people up to date there. I broke when the town was evacuating, as well as the overnight sandbagging efforts. I was the only reporter in Burlington, our competition didn't go there. So the town of Burlington began turning to us.

You are a Jersey boy. How did you wind up in North Dakota?

I ended up in North Dakota, because in TV news you can't start in New York, LA or Philadelphia. You have to start in small towns and work your way up. So after applying in small market places in Florida, Pennsylvania, and Upstate New York, I geared my search to North Dakota, South Dakota, Minnesota, Nebraska, etc. Needless to say, every state in the country received a resume from me. I'm kind of glad to start in a small market. It gives you a chance to make all your mistakes now.

When did the residents of Minot start hearing about possible flooding from the Souris River? How did the station report on it?

Flood talks started in January. It was always a concern because of the amount of snow that North Dakota received. The river was frozen and every city meeting since January, the word "flood" was brought up. So it started to warm up and the Souris River was rising. Residents weren't too concerned. I interviewed one resident who had the river in his backyard and he told me, "I'm not worried about flooding, we'll be fine."

Then June came and then Canada got a major rain storm over the weekend. This was a problem because all that water is going to flow downstream. So the rain water from Canada combined with the already high Souris River was a disaster waiting to happen. Our station was on top of it from the beginning.

As concerned as everyone was about flooding in Minot, a lot of people took it with a grain of salt because Minot had a pretty high levee system. Back in 1969, the town experienced its worse flood on record. So the city went to work putting in a high levee system so flooding would never happen again. So for 40 plus years it didn't flood. But that large rain storm in Canada sent things over the edge.

My colleagues and I were on overnight duty. We got in at 8 a.m. and didn't leave until 6 a.m. the next day. That was every day. My friend Kevin Boughton and I took the first overnight. Our sports reporter was assigned news duty, so he took the next night, and so on. We were running on adrenaline and it was fun. I mean, we were kids who came to a small market to learn this job and next thing we knew we were reporting on something the city will remember forever.

What happened during the Souris River flood? How bad did things get in Minot? How long did it last?

I saw the river when it looked like it was two stories from the top of the levee in Minot, and that was in March. By June 24, the river was at the top of the dike. It looked like a glass of water filled to the top and you're afraid to do anything because you know one move and it's going over. On June 27, the river crested, the clay dikes gave out and the water was spilling over onto city streets and wouldn't look back.

How bad did things get in Minot? It was the worst. Lives were ruined. Homes that were two miles from the river now had two, three feet of water in it. It got to the point where pictures weren't doing it justice. I did a live shot from one place and I was running out of words to describe it. At one point I think I said on live TV, "I don't know what else to say, just look at your screen."

We were broadcasting for 22 hours straight, we were wearing out but the job had to be done. People were turning to us for news and we had to give it to them. As the river began to recede, the damage was being unveiled. I think the water stayed in Minot for about a week and then the water receded. It took about three weeks for it all to go, but then the clean-up process began. Again, we were never desperate for stories at that point.

One of the many angles we took was following residents as they went home – or at least tried too. I'll never forget the emotion in their faces as they saw everything they had ever worked for gone. "We thought they were safe," one person told me. "I mean I'm five blocks from the river, and my house is gone. It's covered in mold. How am I going to explain this to my kids?"

The Souris River was also affecting our water system. So the city put out a boil order alert, which meant in order to drink the water, you had to boil it first to kill any toxins or bacteria. This affected EVERYBODY. Restaurants were now handing out bottles of water, and they were serving their food on paper plates because they couldn't wash them in the dishwasher. We couldn't drink water from a fountain or anything.

What was the scariest moment for you?

As the river was rising, it was taking away streets. If the water even touched the top of the road, that road was getting closed down. So I had one road left that could get me home. One. If that closed down, not just me, but the whole city was screwed.

But I just wanted to make sure I still had an apartment to go home to. I know it sounds selfish and I didn't mean for it to sound that way. But there was that point when I was like, always making sure that river stayed off the road. By the way, the road is 83 Bypass. They call it that because it bypasses the other roads in the city and it gets you from the south of town, to the north of town. I lived on the north side. My apartment wasn't in danger of flooding but again, as long as 83 stayed dry, it would stay open and when I left work at 1 a.m, after working hour number 13, I wanted to make sure I had a pillow to lie on. Luckily I did. Fortunately for me, I never felt in danger, I never felt like I would get hurt or killed or anything. Security officials did a good job of making sure the media was safe, but they also got us close enough to give the viewers up to date information. The only thing I was afraid of was falling asleep at my desk a few times.

What did you learn about yourself as a reporter during the flood coverage?

Basically I learned that 30 hours without sleep is my limit. We had a few days of prepping for the flood crest. Then covering the flood crest, then the aftermath, the clean-up and even six months later we still cover flood angles. It was a rough summer, but one that I learned a lot. I did an interview for a local New Jersey paper, and I used him to vent. I had to talk to someone about what I was going through. As I said before, it was adrenaline at first. Kevin and I were kids in a sense. We were in our first job in Minot, North Dakota. No one heard of this place and suddenly it was making national headlines. KMOT-TV was right there to cover it. Days, weeks and months later, people thanked us for our coverage. They said we did a great job and they couldn't stop watching us. That felt good, because when I got in this business I didn't want to be famous, I didn't want to be rich, I wanted to be good at my job and hearing people thank me for my work made it all worth it.

The other thing that kept me going was my family and friends back home in Jersey. I would receive several calls, texts, Facebook messages, and emails all the time from family, friends, former coworkers, and former classmates asking me how I was doing and that they were thinking of me. That also helped me because I knew that there was a reason I was out here, and that I was being thought of. It took a toll on me to see a city in ruins, and lives in devastation. I couldn't distance myself, I know as a reporter you have to, but you couldn't help but feel for these people. Just the other day, I was going through the stories we did during that time and I turned to my news director and said, "Wow, how the hell did we do it? What a summer."

When did you realize you were in the middle of a national story?

I got a text from friend who said, "hey I read about you guys on Yahoo, or CNN one of them. Good luck out there and stay safe." So I went on CNN and saw the headline which said North Dakota Community Bracing for Flood – or something like that. I couldn't believe it. Here was a town, I had never even thought existed, now making national news and I'm out here covering it.

My mom and dad also kept tabs on it too. They told me, "Hey, I saw Minot on NBC this morning."

Knowing it was a national story helped me bring my game up because you never knew when someone from a national organization would be contacting you. And on one July day, I got a call from the Weather Channel, who told me they wanted my story. So it got fed to a system called News Channel, which is a program all NBC stations use. So any NBC station whether it was in Alaska, New York or Philadelphia could have used my story. I don't know if they did, but I know the Weather Channel used it for sure.

What will you do differently if you have to cover a flood like this again?

Well now that I know what to expect, I think I would use the same approach I used in 2011. However, this time I'll know a little more about the experience. I mean I worked really hard during that time and I don't have any regrets about my coverage, I know what to expect and how to handle it. Since the city of Minot is already preparing itself for flooding in 2012, I am also. Like I said, I'm experienced now. So I think I can do just as good if not better the next time around (hopefully it doesn't happen).

What tips do you have for journalism students if they ever cover a weather disaster like the Minot flood?

Well if you don't feel a rush of energy or enthusiasm when covering a national event or disaster then you should consider another field. Yes, it did get tiring, stressful and mentally draining, but that was later – and most of it was probably due to a lack of sleep. At first however, I was flying high. I mean having people depend on you for information is what this business is about and the fact that I was one of the resources that people listened too was awesome. I mean me, a 24-year-old kid from Jersey who was an average student, was now covering a story that people were talking about.

Wisniewski's Tips for Covering a Flood

- Be approachable and considerate: This is when you talk to real homeowners. I was shocked with how many people wanted to talk. But you figure at that point, they want to vent. But they will cry and be very emotional. Don't treat them like they're just another soundbite for your package or article; treat them like they're longtime friends. It will go a long way. Be respectful to what they're going through.

- Don't plan: If you're covering a disaster, don't expect it to be an easy day. The first day of the flood fight I went into work at 8 a.m. I wanted to get out of work by five because I had plans. I ended up working overnight, the plans were canceled and the girl didn't speak to me again. Little did I know, that would be the beginning of my adventure.

- Stay informed: Know the history of the area you're covering. Have they ever flooded before? If so, how does this flood compare to those in the past? Learn whatever you can about your surroundings. Talk to someone who has lived in the town for a long time. Watch your competition, read the newspaper, Twitter, Facebook. Someone may have something you don't but that doesn't mean you can't enterprise it.

- Work your contacts: Call them all the time. I had the public works director, Burlington mayor, FEMA PIO, and police chief in my phone and called all of them once every two hours. Was I bothering them? Every time I called they had something new they had to get out to our viewers.

- Keep your eyes and ears open: There were so many times when I went out with a story in mind then heard something interesting on the street and said, "Nope, this is my new story angle."

- Think about your safety: Get to where you need to be to get the story or the shot but keep safe. "That water moves fast," one former coworker told me.

Overall, covering a disaster will be a rush. Looking back, I wouldn't trade it for the world. My coworkers and I became closer and I partnered up with other reporters around North Dakota, all of whom I still talk to today. It was intense but I'm proud of the work I did, and if you ever get to cover a disaster and you give it everything you possibly have, there's no better feeling when you lay your head down at night. If you get to lie down.

Hurricanes

If you are a reporter anywhere along the Pacific Coast, Gulf Coast or Atlantic Coast, odds are you will have to cover hurricanes. The National Oceanic & Atmospheric Administration (www.noaa.gov) is your best resource. This government organization predicts the path of a hurricane, its expected landfall and its strength (Categories 1 through 5).

Hurricane forecasting has improved so much in recent years that journalists get a lot of notice about a projected storm. As a result, many reporters in the projected path will find themselves at the supermarket, interviewing people who are stocking up on supplies, or at the home improvement stors, where people are stocking up on plywood and generators.

Kathy Bushouse Burstein covered several major hurricanes while she was a reporter at the South Florida Sun-Sentinel.

If you are deployed to an area away from home, make sure to bring plenty of supplies with you, like enough water and food to last a few days (at least), sunscreen and lots of bug spray.

One of my former colleagues used to talk about how he'd bring extra water with him if he were deployed to the Keys on a hurricane assignment. I would encourage you to bring extra supplies with you to share with people if they need it. Sure, it helps to get people to talk to you, but it's also just the right thing to do.

If your newspaper will allow you to rent an SUV rather than have you drive your own car, do it. No need to risk your own vehicle if you don't have to. Also, you can sleep in the SUV if you have to (like if you can't find a hotel after the storm passes).

Not much will prepare you for what you'll see after a hurricane. I drove to the west coast of Florida after Hurricane Charley – the first of the eight hurricanes to hit the state since 2004 – and was absolutely floored by the sights. Towering metal power poles were snapped in two. Twisted pieces of metal – probably the roof of someone's mobile home – hung from trees. I'll never forget this one sign that I saw, on a road from the highway into Punta Gorda. Someone had taken a mattress and spray painted on it: "Slow down – this is a war zone."

It's OK if what you see bothers you. It should. But you have to push aside whatever feelings you might have until your work is done. For many people, the newspaper is one of the few ways to connect with the outside world after the hurricane passes – you're providing an essential service, so you can't let things get in the way of doing that work.

People will be dazed and in a world of hurt. Be sensitive. Approach them carefully. Ask them how they're doing. Tell them you want to help tell their story. If they decline, say thank you and leave. There will be plenty of other people for you to interview, and there is no need to try and bulldoze someone to talk if they just aren't up to it.

If the hurricane hits in your community, things get a little more complicated. You get frustrated and irritable after days without power. Maybe you cry. The idea of a hot shower becomes all-consuming.

Some perspective helps – I had co-workers whose roofs were torn off their homes, and others who had to figure out how they were going to work and take care of their children. Compared to them, I was extremely lucky.

The first days after a hurricane suck – there's no other word for it. I'm not sure I have any advice on how to get through that, except to say that you will. You work a lot. You get creative when you're home. You play board games when you're not working. You read by flashlight. You drink red wine because it doesn't have to be refrigerated and it helps you get to sleep. You come up with weird ideas to restore some sort of routine: My favorite stupid hurricane trick was to heat up water in a mini-fondue pot, so I had enough warm water to wash my face at night. It was wonderful.

Bottom line: You'll be fine. Covering breaking news like this is why many of us got in the business in the first place. You're providing a real service to your community. It's journalism at its finest. It can be damn near inspiring.

And for my money, there's nothing like that first hot shower after the electricity comes back on.

Reporter **Trymaine D. Lee** survived one of the biggest and most devastating hurricanes in United States history. Lee got hired by The Times-Picayune in New Orleans just a few months before Hurricane Katrina slammed the city in August 2005. The storm was one of the most devastating to ever hit the United States and caused untold misery and political fallout.

Journalists in Louisiana and Mississippi worked under dreadful conditions, with little sleep and often suffered devastating personal losses. Still, they had to tell the story of the storm.

Here is one of the stories Lee wrote in the days after Hurricane Katrina. It appeared in The Times-Picayune on Sept. 1, 2005:

Lucrece Phillips' sleepless nights are filled with the images of dead babies and women, and young and old men with tattered T-shirts or graying temples, all of whom she saw floating along the streets of the Lower 9th Ward. The deaths of many of her neighbors who chose to brave the hurricane from behind the walls of their Painter Street homes shook tears from Phillips' bloodshot eyes Tuesday, as a harrowing tale of death and survival tumbled from her lips.

"The rescuers in the boats that picked us up had to push the bodies back with sticks," Phillips said sobbing. "And there was this little baby. She looked so perfect and so beautiful. I just wanted to scoop her up and breathe life back into her little lungs. She wasn't bloated or anything, just perfect."

A few hours after Phillips, 42, and five members of her family and a friend had been rescued from the attic of her second-story home in the 2700 block of Painter Street, she broke down with a range of emotions. Joy, for surviving the killer floods; pain, for the loss of so many lives; and uncertainty, about the well-being of her family missing in the city's most ravaged quarters.

In a darkened lobby of the downtown Hyatt hotel turned refuge, she hugged an emergency worker closely; a handful of his sweaty blue T-shirt rippling from each of her fists.

She had barely gotten out a fifth thank you when the emergency worker whispered into her ear that "it was going to be OK," and that "it was our job to save lives."

Six months after the storm, Lee wrote down the top five things he learned from covering Hurricane Katrina. Here is what he wrote:

- Pack a personal survival kit in a book bag or duffle bag. Stuff it with some snacks and bottled water if possible, first-aid stuff, toiletries and a couple pair of underwear and socks. Guard it with your life. Keep it in arm's reach. Especially a bar of soap. If the worst case scenario hits, you might not know where your next meal or shower will come from. Our office was flooded and the paper evacuated. I was on assignment in the field when they left. Most of my things were on the second floor. Luckily, I had a bag with some soap, a tooth brush with me, a pillow and a sandwich. When hell and high water came, my little bag made things just a bit easier.

- Be safe but go with your instincts. During Hurricane Katrina, the story presented itself – whether it was the flooded streets, the faces of the first responders or the hungry and stranded residents searching for a way out of the city. As adventurous as I had to be to get the story, I was cautious most of the time. At points I was alone and away from anyone who could contact my next of kin if I'd drowned or caught a stray bullet. But if I had to do it all over, I would push the envelope a bit more. I would go deeper and into the dark, scary places. When tragedy strikes and people are dying, we as journalists need to go to the mountain tops or the bottom of the sea to tell the people's story.

- Be in the chaos but not of the chaos. It's easy to allow emotions to take over your sensibilities. Emotions are good but harness them and use them to your advantage. But never panic. Be cool and understand why you are in the middle of hell. You are there to gather the most accurate information as possible and translate to those affected by the disaster or those fortunate enough to be far-far away from it. Let your emotions guide you to the heart of the story, to the people who bleed just like you. But never allow them to unnerve you. You'll be an ineffective mess when readers and your fellow reporters will need you most.

- Don't overthink the situation. Become part of your environment and allow what you are seeing, smelling, hearing and tasting guide your stories. Think about the supplementary information for your story later, but let the "here and now" color your canvas.

- Don't believe everything you hear and some of the stuff you see. When interviewing sources, understand that they are likely under extreme stress and might not be thinking clearly. During Katrina, communications were down, and information and lots of rumors were spreading strictly by word of mouth. We learned the hard way that much of what we were hearing about rapes and murders were false. I personally spoke to people claiming to witness throat slicings and rapes. Be sure to word that stuff carefully once you are crafting your story. Cover your bases. You might not be able to find the truth, but be sure to do as much fact checking as humanly possible.

A few weeks after Hurricane Katrina, the student newspaper at Rowan University, where I teach, interviewed Lee. Here is the story from Rowan's weekly student newspaper, The Whit.

Reporting in the Ruins of New Orleans
The Whit
September 15, 2005
Steve Stirling

Most view death, hope, desperation and joy as experiences that are part of the journey of life – things that build and mold a person's character as the seasons change and the years go by.

Some experience a lifetime of this in just a week's time.

Trymaine D. Lee, a 26-year-old 2003 graduate of Rowan University, is a police reporter for the New Orleans Times-Picayune. In the wake of Hurricane Katrina he has seen all of these emotions. He has seen the darkest side of the human struggle; the desperation, destruction and despair. And in the deepest corners of this tragedy, he

71

has seen light and benevolence in the people of New Orleans.

"It's been humbling and horrible," said Lee, who is currently taking some time off after spending the past two-and-a-half weeks entrenched in New Orleans. "Once I took a few days off, the emotions really weighed in."

As a student at Rowan, Lee majored in journalism, was a staff writer at The Whit and interned at the Philadelphia Daily News. He began working on the police beat at the Times-Picayune last April, and while he has seen his share of tragedy in the crime-stricken city, it pales in comparison to his experiences since Aug. 27.

"As a journalist this is the World Series, this is the biggest story I will likely cover in my lifetime," said Lee. "As a human it's really hard to see this type of pain and struggle. Seeing a city like this on its knees, it's really sad."

The Escape

Since he came from the Northeast, Lee was unfamiliar to the almost routine preparations that take place along the Gulf Coast in the event of a hurricane. More than a day before the storm hit, his colleagues at the Times-Picayune were already talking about turning their newsroom into a storm shelter. Before long, he was packing a bag and moving into his workplace with co-workers and their families.

When Hurricane Katrina roared through the city of New Orleans from late Aug. 28 to Aug. 29, Lee says it was short but fierce.

"Sunday night the wind started; the storm hadn't even come in yet but you could feel it, it was coming," Lee said. "Early Monday it came through. The winds were ridiculous, you could hear them, but by 1:30 p.m., or so, things calmed down."

Once the storm calmed down, Lee offered to relieve a co-worker who had been covering the hourly updates being given by emergency officials at City Hall in downtown New Orleans. He hadn't returned to the office that briefly sheltered him since leaving for City Hall.

"They were supposed to pick me up the next morning," Lee said. "They never came. By that point most communication in the city was down. It wasn't until I heard from a friend in New Jersey that I found out that [The Times-Picayune] had left."

Shortly thereafter, as floodwaters flowed in from breaches in the city's levee system, City Hall was evacuated. Lee and everyone else waded across waist-high water to the storm-battered Hyatt Hotel across the street.

Shattered windows and dim lights marked the scene for one of the most emotional interviews of Lee's career.

It was there that he spoke with Lucrece Phillips, a 42-year-old New Orleans resident, who tearfully recalled to Lee the deaths of neighbors who tried to weather the storm, and watching rescue workers push the floating bodies of the perished aside as they took her to safety.

"Working as a police reporter I have that tear in my eye a lot. You see a lot of violence and crime," Lee said. "That was the first time I really broke down. You could see the pain in her eyes and the death on her face."

Fortunately for Lee, he and a friend were able to flag down a truck that took him to safety. But the worst was still coming for New Orleans as the flood waters continued to rise, and the job of Lee and his fellow reporters was far from over.

The Convention Center

Lee returned to the beleaguered city to a human sea of desperation and despair. Tens of thousands had gathered at the New Orleans Convention Center with no guidance and were running low on food, water and hope.

"A whole population had gathered there hoping for some kind of refuge, but there was no one there. No police, no officials, no government," Lee said.

It wasn't until Friday, four days after the storm hit, that the federal government was able to get to the convention center with food and water. By then, looting had broken out all over the city, something that Lee says was overly criminalized by the government and the media.

"You had these people that were stereotyped as 'thugs' looting, but a lot of them were looting food and water, sharing it with their neighbors, giving it to the elderly, just trying to survive," he said.

Lee was surprised that the situation didn't escalate any further, and said it was a testament to the spirit of the people of New Orleans.

"The craziest part about it was that many of these people had lost their entire families and walked miles through neck-high water looking for some kind of refuge, then getting here and finding nothing," he said. "The resilience of these people is amazing."

Diamonds in the Rough

Seeping through the cracks of flooded houses is brightness, a compassionate light that shines toward a future for a city that has hit rock bottom. New Orleans may be a city wrought with misfortune, but Lee sees hope within the people of the city.

"Right now you have neighbors sharing water and food, you have children and babies that are somehow not losing their minds." After this, he said, "These people can rise above anything."

Lee came across a woman recently that told him how she found an elderly couple walking down the sidewalk. They were both in desperate need of medication for epilepsy and heart conditions, so she took them back to her neighborhood, where remaining neighbors had gathered in a small community.

A Rastafarian man wrote down the medical prescriptions of everyone in the neighborhood, then broke into a Rite-Aid pharmacy and filled each of them, insuring the well-being of many in the community.

"These are the looters," Lee said, "These are the people the governor is saying to take out by any means necessary."

He went on to clarify that he wasn't advocating criminal acts, but that many of these 'looters' were just trying to survive and help others.

"If that isn't brotherhood and communal connection, then what is?" he said.

After 'hitting a wall,' Lee said he's ready for a break and will be coming home to New Jersey to visit his mother in the next few days. But while the experience may have left him weathered and emotionally drained, Lee said the story isn't difficult to tell.

"You know how they say truth is stranger than fiction? Well you don't have to add anything to this. An entire city was evacuated. An entire city packed up and relocated; it's all there," he said.

Sometimes you don't have to add pain and passion. The story just tells itself.

10 Tips on *Covering Bad Weather and Disasters*

- Don't tether yourself to a building and then stand in the middle of a hurricane while reporting live on television. It doesn't matter that Dan Rather got his start this way. You will blow away or get hurt. Or just look stupid.

- Do not wear flip-flops to cover a wildfire! Wear proper footwear and clothing to cover bad weather or natural disasters – jeans, sturdy shoes, a hat and a good jacket or rain poncho.

- When a hurricane or blizzard is predicted, pack a bag with essentials and keep it with you in the office. Don't keep it in your car because the parking lot may flood or get snowed in.

- Put gas in your car and get out money from the ATM. When the power goes out, ATMs stop working and so do gas pumps.

- Get your family settled and put your possessions in safe places when a hurricane is predicted. You can't do your job if you are worried about your family. Have a plan for how to reach them after the storm hits, if you have to work.

- Do not drive through flooded areas. That is how most people die in floods – their cars get swamped and they get swept away.

- Watch out for downed power lines after big storms. You could get electrocuted.

- Do NOT quote people who describe a tornado as sounding "like a train." Everyone does that. It is very clichéd. Ask more questions.

- Be safe but go with your instincts.

- Don't believe all the hype. Many of the stories reported after Hurricane Katrina turned out to be wild rumors. Get the facts. Get multiple sources.

In-Class Activity/Homework

1. List the kind of news-making weather stories and natural disasters that occur in your area.

2. What kinds of buildings (like schools) and systems (like railroads) could be affected in your area during bad weather or a natural disaster?

3. Find the website for your state's Emergency Management office. What is the phone number? Who is in charge during a weather crisis or natural disaster?

4. Go to the website for the federal National Oceanic and Atmospheric Administration. Are there any tropical storms or hurricanes currently in the forecast?

5. Look up the Saffir-Simpson scale for measuring hurricanes. What are the characteristics of Category 3, 4 and 5 hurricanes?

6. What are the names of the hurricanes for this upcoming season?

7. What is the location, phone number and website for your local National Weather Service office? Are there any severe weather alerts for today?

8. In your area, what are the rivers, creeks or other bodies of water that are likely to flood? For instance, New Jersey has the Middle Atlantic River Forecast.

9. Go to the Federal Emergency Management website (fema.gov). Who is the director?

10. What items should you have in your emergency kit in case of a disaster?

Journalist Q&A

Courtesy of the author

Antigone Barton

Where do you work?
Self-employed/Between fellowships

What is your beat or job title?
I am a freelance journalist who spent eight years covering health, justice and environment issues for the Palm Beach Post in South Florida. During the last seven years I wrote extensively about the AIDS epidemic in the US and abroad. A former teacher, I spent a year in Zambia as a Knight Health Journalism fellow through the International Center for Journalists (ICFJ), working with journalists there to develop in-depth health reporting. I spent 2010-2011 at Harvard University where I studied global health research and ethics as a Nieman Journalism Fellow.

Where did you go to college and what was your degree?
Virginia Commonwealth University, Master of Science, Mass Communication; State University of New York/College at Old Westbury, BA Comparative History Ideas and Culture

Did you work on your college newspaper or online news website?
No.

Did you have any internships? If so, where and what did you do?
Interned at NPR affiliate, and business radio station

When and where was your first journalism job? What is one thing you learned from it?
The now defunct South Florida Newspaper Network as news editor of the Boca Thursday paper. I learned three things that all were important when I started working on projects later on: how to lay out a newspaper, the haiku of headline writing, how to edit a story.

What was the hardest part of your first journalism job?
Nothing. I was surrounded by supportive people who were good mentors. My second job however, as a copy editor on a small daily was grueling –

monotonous and blinding. I have needed glasses ever since that year spent six inches from a computer screen.

What advice would you give to a journalism major?

Know why you cover what you cover. Follow issues and events that are important to you, that move you, that you want to know more about. Look for links between local and global events so that you can better understand and present news in an understandable, relevant and comprehensive context. Don't settle for answers that don't make sense to you. Identify your prejudices and learn what you need know to rid yourself of them. If you work for an outlet that is not interested in covering issues of honest concern to its readers, aim higher.

Many beginning journalists get very nervous about their first assignments. Did you get nervous and how did you cope?

When I began to work as a reporter I was worried I would get back to the office, or reach the end of the time I could contact people only to find I didn't have what I needed to tell the story I had spent the day (or night) trying to get. I never left a scene or meeting, or hung up the phone until I had asked everything I thought I would want to know if I was reading the story.

What is the worst part about being a journalist?

Realizing in 2008, when my newspaper offered buyouts to everyone who had worked there five years or more that I couldn't continue to work for a quality daily newspaper, was hard. The experiences and freedom I have enjoyed since, however, more than made up for that loss.

What is the best part?

Retaining the ability and desire to write stories that I care about and that I believe people should know about.

What would you tell yourself at the beginning of your career, if you could go back in time?

To believe in my instincts, not to sell myself short and not to be scared to move on – to better newspapers, different outlets, different ways to tell stories.

Chapter 6
Press Conferences and Speeches

Courtesy of Cathy A. Cramer

Cops catch a killer. A politician announces her candidacy for president. A star athlete signs a multi-million dollar professional sports contract.

These are all topics of press conferences and speeches. As a reporter, it is your job to be there to cover these events. Sometimes press conferences and speeches are boring and canned. Other times they crackle with excitement. Either way, you need to get the story and get it correctly.

This can be hard if you don't know anything about the topic. But planning ahead can save you time and effort.

The main thing to realize about press conferences and speeches is that they are PLANNED events. They are pre-packaged, pseudo-events. This doesn't mean they aren't newsworthy – they are. It is just that the news of the press conference may turn out to be different from what the organizers intended.

For instance, I have attended "press conferences" where I was the only reporter who showed up. And sometimes in politics, a candidate's staff will crowd the meeting room to make it look like there are more supporters than in reality. It is the journalist's job to report what is really going on, not the public relations version.

Press conferences are aimed at the media, and there is usually time for journalists to ask questions. Press conferences are held when something needs to be announced. Speeches can be for any kind of audience and it is never certain whether the speaker will have time to answer questions or not.

Speeches can be history making. Who among us journalists doesn't wish we got to cover Martin Luther King Jr.'s "I Have a Dream" speech about civil rights or President John F. Kennedy's inauguration? Those speeches were communication elevated to history. Now, imagine if the reporter covering those speeches got the quotes wrong or missed the point entirely.

The way to avoid that is to be prepared. If you have to cover a speech by a local politician, do a quick check of your news organization's archives to see what has been written about that politician.

For the most part, the topics of press conferences and speeches are straight forward. If Coca-Cola invents a new soft-drink flavor, company executives will hold a press conference to announce it. If an author is giving a speech, a press release will be sent out about it.

Two things to keep in mind are the **topic** and the **speaker**. Any time the president of the United States makes a speech, or holds a press conference, it is news, even if the president doesn't have much to say. The same is not true of the local tax collector, unless the local tax collector announces he's quitting to audition for "American Idol." THAT would be news. Lots of people can hold news conferences and it doesn't always mean it is news. That is up to you and your editors to decide.

I estimate that 50 percent of being a good journalist is showing up in the right place at the right time. That is true for press conferences and speeches. It doesn't matter how prepared you are if you are in the wrong meeting room or stuck in cross-town traffic. Try to get there early.

I was a reporter in North Carolina at the Fayetteville Observer, which covered the Fort Bragg U.S. Army Base. An Army sergeant with a grudge against his colleagues opened fire on them while they exercised outside in the early morning. He killed one soldier and injured others. A few Green Berets jogging by wrestled the gun away from the sergeant with their bare hands to stop him from shooting anyone else. It was an exciting and sad story.

I got sent out to Fort Bragg early in the morning after my editor heard about the shooting, so I started reporting, along with other journalists on my staff. By the early afternoon, the national media – reporters from ABC, CBS, NBC, the New York Times, etc. – began arriving at Fort Bragg to cover the story we local reporters had already been working on for hours.

A press conference was scheduled. I got there early, before many other people, and got a seat in the front row. I was glad I did, even though I had to wait nearly one hour. The room quickly filled up with reporters and military officials. The national reporters began shouting out questions and I got a sense of how more experienced reporters covered a story. It was both exciting and intimidating. It felt like the national reporters were going to completely take over the story.

Luckily, the five Special Forces soldiers – known as Green Berets – spoke at the press conference and gave a detailed account of how they subdued the sergeant. Here is an excerpt from that story:

Five Special Forces soldiers tackled a gunman bare-handed Friday morning and sat on him until military police arrived.

Army officials said the gunman – identified as Sgt. William J. Kreutzer – had just shot 19 soldiers, killing one. He was armed with a pistol and two rifles. The Green Berets were unarmed, dressed only in their shorts and T-shirts.

Staff Sgt. Anthony Minor said he and the other Green Berets did not stop to consider the danger.

"Instincts took over," he said...

They were running up Bastogne Drive about 6:30 a.m. when they heard loud pops. They stopped and listened. They heard the "ping" of bullets hitting concrete.

Sgt. 1st Class Edward Mongold looked toward the trees. Through the darkness and the fog, he could make out a soldier dressed in a camouflage uniform, standing near the tree line. The man was shooting toward a battalion of 1,300 soldiers in the bowl-shaped athletic field below.

Mongold and two of the Special Forces soldiers crept up behind him. Suddenly, he turned and began shooting at them.

Mongold dove at the man's knees. Minor landed on the man's back and shoulders.

The man put up a fierce struggle, Minor said.

"It was a fight for his life. It was a fight for all our lives," Minor said.

It is hard not to be intimidated by more experienced reporters if you find yourself in the middle of a national event. But take a deep breath and listen closely to the speech or press conference.

A trick at press conferences is to listen to the other reporters and write down the answers they get. It doesn't matter who does the asking (unless you are a high-paid network TV star). The answers are what matters.

Unless, of course, the person holding the press conference decides to berate the journalist asking the questions. That happened to reporter James L. Rosica when he was working at the Tallahasee Democrat newspaper in Florida. Rosica was assigned to cover a speech by legendary comedian Bill Cosby. Instead, he wound up getting yelled at by the TV dad. Rosica wrote this essay about what happened when he met Cosby.

Bill Cosby bit his lower lip as he looked over the sea of faces, each wearing a cap and gown. "Help me, Class of 2003," he said. "I'm worried about you."

Actually Cos, I thought later, I'm worried about you.

Cosby was in the middle of a commencement speech turned tongue-lashing at Florida A&M, the Sunshine State's historically black university in Tallahassee. His brother Russell, famed from Cosby's many stand-up routines, was one of the graduates, having gone to college late in life. My editors at the Tallahassee Democrat assigned me to cover the event for a front-page story. "Have fun with it," they said. Fun, however, later turned into me being yelled at by 'America's Dad.'

What we didn't realize was Cosby was just beginning a series of controversial speeches critical of blacks who, in his words, were "dragging our culture down." I scribbled furiously in my notebook as I heard him complain about young men who call women "bitches and 'hos" and refer to each other using the N-word. He railed against young women who had children outside marriage.

As he wrapped up his remarks to applause and a few puzzled-looking faces, the school's spokeswoman wrangled me and some other reporters into a post-speech press conference. One of the television reporters tugged at my arm as we walked: "Did you hear him drop the N-bomb? Hello!"

We all looked at each other as microphones were being duct-taped on the lectern; who was going to broach the issue first? After a few softball questions, that same television reporter tried, but Cosby brushed her off. I immediately followed up: "I think what she means is, you used some tough words out there, and ...."

I never got a chance to finish; Cosby yelled at me for 10 minutes for what he not-so-subtly suggested was an inappropriate question. I didn't understand, he told me. "I understand," I said, lamely trying to defuse him. "My dad's an Ed.D. too and we always have these kinds of conversations." He would have none of it. "Well then, you obviously weren't listening to him either!"

University supporters had been standing in the back of the room; their eyes narrowed as they stared at me withering under Cosby's relentless harangue. At some point, I felt a hand on my shoulder. The spokeswoman was behind me, looking terrified. "Yeah, we need to get you out of here," she whispered. As she led me out, I could see Camille, Cosby's wife, quietly talking to him. Suddenly, he burst out, "Well I mean, who IS this guy?!"

I drove back to the office, trying to figure out what happened. I supposed he thought I was going to criticize the speech, then decided on a pre-emptive strike. Who knows. I typed my story, careful not to show my own anger and leaving out any mention of "bitches and 'hos" so I wouldn't stroke out my family-friendly editor.

The next morning, Cosby's publicist called me to say how much "Bill really appreciated the story."

Uh, were you at that press conference, I asked. The flack defended the source of his paycheck, suggesting it was my fault for riling his client. I cut short the call, then muttered to a colleague what I wanted to tell the guy: "Tell America's Dad to go f--- himself ...."

Here is Rosica's upshot on a press conference that becomes controversial:

- Keep your cool, don't respond to incivility with incivility (or, the louder they get, the softer you should get) and head back to the newsroom.

- Make sure your editors know what happened and then write it straight (unless your editor wants all the conflict in there).

If you are unsure about the topic, do some quick online research. If there is no time for that, ask the person who organized the speech or press conference for background information. Often there is also a written program from which you can draw information. Take copies of any handouts that are provided by the organizers of the events and get the business card of one of the organizers in case you need to call later with questions.

Many speeches – especially those given by politicians – are photocopied and available for the press ahead of time. This saves you writer's cramp. But follow along in the speech to see if the speaker varies or ad libs from the text. Observe how many times the speech or press conference is interrupted by applause or protests. Mark that in your notes.

It may seem obvious, but bring batteries for your digital recorder and test it beforehand to make sure it works. And even if you bring a recording device, take notes just in case. It is better to have more notes and detail than none if the recorder stops working.

Lisa Colangelo is a reporter for the New York Daily News. She is a proponent of placing a few extra pens and pads of paper in your bag before you leave the newsroom.

"I know it sounds silly but after almost 20 years as a reporter I sometimes run to press conferences with a notebook that is full and I have to scribble notes on a press release - which is lame," Colangelo said.

She works in the high-pressure and fiercely competitive arena of New York newspapers and politics. Not only must Colangelo get the story and get it right, she must also try and get it first to beat the competition.

While covering City Hall in a small town might be laid back and predictable, nothing could be further from the truth at New York City mayoral press conferences.

For New York Mayor Michael Bloomberg, press conferences are a way to highlight announcements or special city programs, Colangelo said. He knows he can answer questions from the press at the end of the announcement.

"But first you have to get through the announcement the Mayor wants to make. Sometimes the announcement itself is very newsworthy – the city is adding 1,200 cops to the force. But sometimes it's a ribbon cutting at an underwear factory at a new industrial park in Queens or a mentoring program in Manhattan."

Doug Elfman is an entertainment columnist for the Las Vegas Review-Journal. He interviews celebrities, goes to parties, attends nightclub openings and frequently covers press conferences of high-profile people. His job sounds like a dream, but he got there through hard work, including years spent as a cops and courts reporter.

"Covering hard news gets you in the habit of thinking like a news person who asks impossible questions of people face to face. It makes you fearless," Elfman said.

"Since I was able to once ask a man: 'Why did you rape your kids?' it made it much easier to say to Britney Spears years later: 'You say you're a virgin, but you own two houses with Justin (Timberlake)?'

Elfman covered the impromptu press conference of a wealthy

businessman and turned it into a feature story. Here is how he got the story:

"It was my day off when Steve Wynn — the billionaire hotelier who was going blind — asked reporters to meet him in a majestic suite in his Wynn hotel. He wanted to talk about his Vegas wedding, coming up the next Saturday.

This was a big deal. Wynn and his ex-wife Elaine had been fixtures in Vegas for decades. He was the Republican who built luxurious hotels; Elaine was the Democrat who championed public schools — that old cliché. But abruptly, Wynn, 69, divorced Elaine and got engaged to a 47-year-old mystery woman from Europe.

To prep for the press conference, I went over his background online, reminding myself: This is the kind of person I will be talking with.

As a kid growing up in Utica, New York, Wynn took over his gambling dad's bingo parlors, parlayed that into a small fortune, then moved to Vegas in the 1960s with Elaine.

He kick-started his Vegas career by renovating smoky hotel-casinos. Eventually, he built the opulent Bellagio and Wynn-Encore resorts. If you've seen "Ocean's 11," you've seen the Bellagio and a fictionalized, less gregarious version of Wynn, as portrayed by Andy Garcia. Wynn is grandiose and impetuous. Supposedly, he once caused a ripple in investor confidence by singing in a boardroom. Apparently, investors get wigged out when a CEO performs a happy tune.

Wynn had the foresight to introduce Vegas to luxury hotels, celebrity-chef restaurants and Cirque du Soleil. But now, this visionary suffered a degenerative eye disease. If you were to put a straw to your pupil and squint, you would see the world as Wynn would — a narrow tunnel, narrowing.

When he built the Wynn hotel in 2005, he gave the casino walls textured surfaces that feel exquisite to the touch — a valuable sense for a wealthy blind man. In 2006, he was showing off one of his $85 million Picassos to Barbara Walters when he accidentally poked an elbow through the canvas.

Before the press conference, I engaged in my secret interviewing technique that I never tell other journalists about: I scrutinized YouTube interviews of my subject to get a feel for his speaking pattern and body language; to see if he's a proper fellow, a gutter mouth, a rambler, a genuine person, an evader, a regular guy or a prima donna; and to get a sense of when it's useful to let him babble or to interrupt.

I called insider sources to query: "Are there any questions you think I should ask him?" They told me the latest naughty gossip but nothing I didn't already know.

As it turned out, I was the only person at the press conference who asked good questions, because the other dozen or so journalists were broadcasters.

Wynn began with a simple statement that Saturday's wedding would be fun. Since it was big news that he was marrying this secretive European woman

named Andrea Hissom, I asked a lot of questions about their relationship —
questions I would ask him if I were his friend or therapist:

How did you meet? (At a restaurant in the French Riviera, through mutual
rich friends.) Why do you love her? ("Andrea wakes up every morning full of
happiness and looking to have fun." He was also drawn to her Euro sensibilities
and her ability to have friendships with "girlfriends and boyfriends.") Why does
she love you? ("I know I've tried very hard to make her look at me in heroic
terms — as every guy does.")

Why didn't she come to this press conference? (She didn't want to become a
public figure.) Does Andrea plan to follow Elaine's footsteps as a major presence
at your hotels? (He didn't know, but his ex-wife, Elaine, was still a decisive force
at his hotels, as the divorce was amicable.) What do you and Andrea do for fun?
(Hang with other rich and powerful friends at restaurants and VIP parties.)
What rich and famous people are attending, or performing at, the wedding? (He
refused to divulge.) Why didn't you invite me to your wedding? (He laughed and
said the guest list was full.)

For my lady readers, I asked: Who designed Andrea's dress and shoes? (He
didn't know, but a publicist told me later.) And how did he propose? (I don't
remember what he said, but it must have been dull or evasive because I didn't
put it in my column.)

I took notes by hand while recording the hour sit-down. Broadcasters kept
asking super idiotic questions about Wynn's hatred of President Obama and
unions. All Wynn ever wants to talk about to the press is Obama and unions.
So I politely sat through Wynn's usual spiels and then interrupted at the
right moments, and redirected him constantly back into a real and flowing
conversation. As the best homicide detectives will tell you, people always reveal
more facts and emotions in friendly-toned, anxiety-free conversations than they
do in rigid Q&A formats.

My instinct was to lead my column with how he met his fiancée at that
French Riviera restaurant. But Wynn exclaimed that his wedding would be
way more fun than the royal wedding of Prince William and Kate that same
weekend in London, so that was just extravagant enough to steal the lead. In
retrospect, I wish I had led with the French Riviera and written the column as a
chronology of their relationship. Live and learn."

10 Tips on *Covering Speeches and Press Conferences*

- Make sure you have a pen, paper and a recording device. Check before you leave.

- Get the exact location of the press conference ahead of time. There is nothing worse than being late to an announcement or speech because you are in the wrong meeting room.

- Get there early so you can grab a good seat and see who else is there.

- Consider your questions carefully. At many news conferences, the bigwigs usually answer a limited number of questions. Don't waste one of them on something you can easily answer with a little legwork, such as: "Senator, how many terms have you served?"

- Ask yourself: What is the REAL story? This may be different than the "news" of the press conference.

- Do your homework before the press conference. Make sure you know who is speaking and what the topic is about.

- Be careful with the prepared text. Reporters are often given copies of speeches, which is helpful. But speakers often ad-lib. So read the printed page to make sure that's what the speaker really says before you quote from it.

- Be ready to file your story. News conferences and speeches often result in breaking news. Be ready to write a short story quickly. Make sure you get some of the most useful quotes down verbatim so you don't have to go back to the tape right away. Dog-ear your notebook page so you can find the quotes easily.

- Get reaction from people in the crowd (NOT other reporters). That is often the freshest, best material.

- If you can, hang around after it's over. You might be able to get a few minutes of one-on-one time with the candidate or chat up a detective who will give you the real deal on the murder case.

In-Class Activity/Homework

Go online and find audio or video of a famous speech from a politician or activist. Some suggestions include:

- Winston Churchill's "We Shall Fight on The Beaches" or "Never Give In" speeches
- President Franklin Delano Roosevelt's speech after the Pearl Harbor attack
- Dr. Martin Luther King Jr.'s "I Have a Dream Speech"
- The inaugural speech of President John F. Kennedy
- President Ronald Reagan's "Tear Down This Wall" or "Shuttle Challenger" speeches
- The inaugural speech of President Barack Obama

Use the space below and on the next page, or a computer and mouse, to take notes on the speech. Try to get as many full quotes as you can. Sum up the speech. Now go back and find the text of the speech. Compare your notes to the text and see the accuracy of your quotes. If your accuracy is low, keep practicing and listen to more speeches.

Journalist Q&A

Courtesy of Tanya Kenevich

Tanya Kenevich

What is your name?
Tanya Marie "Short and Sweet" Kenevich

Where do you work?
Kates-Boylston Publications

What is your job title?
I am editor of a death-care publications company. We focus on trade publications for funeral directors, funeral home owners, cremationists, embalmers, death-care consultants, the list goes on.

Where did you go to college and what was your degree?
I went to Rowan University; my degree was a bachelor's in journalism.

Did you work on your college newspaper or online news website?
Did I work at my college newspaper? Hell, I RAN the college newspaper. I think it's very important for future writers to get their hands dirty and write anywhere they can – whether it is working for the college newspaper, the local small newspaper or even blogging, it's best to continue to hone your talents and make them better. I'm a big advocate for that, because in journalism, if you talk the talk, you better walk the walk – that is, have clips to show. And good ones!

Did you have any internships? If so, where and what did you do?
I had an internship at Curious Parents magazine in South Jersey. I did features articles there, as well as some data entry and calendar updating. It was about 10 hours a week, but it gave me a good look at how a publishing company worked.

When and where was your first journalism job? What is one thing you learned from it?
My first journalism job was a couple of months after I graduated in the summer of 2006. I was working at Waldenbooks to keep myself busy and make a few bucks and I was interviewing when I wasn't working. I found a trade publication company for the natural product industry on (a job search

website) and I decided to interview for it. Thanks to my clips from the college newspaper, I got it.

What was the hardest part of your first journalism job?
It's hard being the lowest part of the totem pole, but hey, you have to start somewhere. No one is going to pay you $60k right out of college to write. Let me repeat that: NO ONE is going to pay you $60k right out of college to write. You have to take your blows and show what you have to offer. You'll do the jobs no one wants to do. You might have to get coffee and do "assistant" things. You might have to do data entry. But if you are really passionate about it, you'll just suck it up and do it. Good things will happen if you just focus on your dream.

Many beginning journalists get very nervous about their first assignments. Did you get nervous and how did you cope?
Try to understand that you are interviewing PEOPLE. Yes, these people might be famous, or have a lot of money or be very well known, but they are still people. Talk to them in a courteous matter, but still show in your own way that you want "just the facts, ma'am." Although I do find that some banter loosens up who you're talking to. If you make your interviewee comfortable, they are bound to say much more. Also, do your research before an interview! Don't do in blind and go, "So, what do you do again?" It's fine to question certain facts to the interviewee to make sure, but if you don't seem like you know what you're doing, no one is going to take you seriously. And if you still really don't know what you're taking about, even after you've tried, FAKE IT.

What is the worst part about being a journalist?
It's busy. It's stressful. People will criticize your work. Sometimes that's hard to hear, but most of the time, people are trying to help you become a better writer.

What is the best part?
Having my name on great works of art! People respect that and will go, "YOU'RE Tanya Kenevich?" It's pretty cool and it never gets old!

What advice would you give to a journalism major?
If you don't take the time and write, don't expect much. This is not an industry where you are just handed money or fame because you are nice. Write as much as you can, anywhere you can and also read! Reading is a great way to see different voices in writing, and that helps to create your own.

What would you tell yourself at the beginning of your career, if you could go back in time?

It's okay to have a quick cry in the bathroom when things get too hectic. It doesn't mean you are weak – it means you are not a robot.

Chapter 7
Parades and Protests

Courtesy of Lori M. Nichols

At some point in their careers, most reporters will have to cover a parade, protest or festival. News organizations love these stories because they provide readers and viewers with colorful details, quirky characters and drama. Think of the residents of New Orleans who spent months working on Mardi Gras floats – even after Hurricane Katrina destroyed much of the city. Or the sticky faces of little kids. And for drama, flash back to the thousands of protestors facing down the military in Egypt during the 2011 "Arab Spring."

These events are chock-full of vivid sights to see and interesting people to interview.

But these stories can be done badly, and often are. Because parades and festivals happen so frequently, the coverage can spiral into clichés. Paragraphs about bright red fire trucks and tykes watching the Ferris Wheel at the fair tire quickly.

Some reporters simply can't stand these assignments because they feel so hokey. I like them, but they do get repetitive. For instance, after the third time I covered the Turkey Festival in Hoke County, N.C., I was starting to run out of adjectives to describe the guy dressed as a turkey and the taste of turkey nuggets. But I had to persevere, since the festival is one of the biggest events in the town of Raeford, N.C. To cover it sloppily or not at all would have been blasphemy to the townspeople and would have cost me my job. So I ate some more nuggets and went about reporting and writing.

Protests can be tricky because of the danger and also because there is so much chaos and shouting. It can be hard to figure out what's going on and stereotypes are easy to portray.

But instead of describing protesters as law-breaking no-goodniks, spend the day with one to get a different perspective. And perspective is the key here – look at these stories from a different angle, not a clichéd one.

When covering a parade, protest or festival, the first thing a reporter should do is just spend 30 minutes walking around and taking in the scene. Look, listen and write notes. After that, focus on someone involved in the event to interview. For instance, look for a family member of the high school marching band, or a protester holding a clever sign. Next, move on to people watching the events, such as families lining the street or police blocking the protesters from a building. Interview them.

All the while, take in the sights and sounds, especially the energy and color.

Here is a typical parade story that I wrote for the Palm Beach Post. It was the 50th anniversary of a town called Palm Beach Shores.

PALM BEACH SHORES – Some people like to celebrate their 50th birthdays quietly, with reflection and reminiscence. Not so the town of Palm Beach Shores. This community on Singer Island threw itself a big party, complete with lots of noisemakers and a giant cake.

The birthday party kicked off Saturday with a parade through town. Shriners rode their tiny tin lizzies. The Boy Scouts marched in step and ladies in Arabian attire rode their horses. The town's fire trucks led the way with lights flashing, sirens blaring and horns blowing.

Joe and Rose Graham of Oceanside, N.Y., stood and smiled as the parade passed them by. They vacation in Palm Beach Shores every year. For Joe Graham, the fire trucks were a glimpse of his past. He was a firefighter in the New York City borough of Brooklyn for 27 years, working on a pumper truck.

While others in the crowd held their ears, Joe Graham stood unfazed by the horns and sirens.

"You get used to it," he said.

Al and Hannah Blake have had the past 50 years to get used to each other. The Palm Beach Shores residents are celebrating their 50th anniversary this year and rode in a car during the parade, dressed in a tuxedo and top hat and a wedding gown and veil.

After the parade, they stood near town hall and shook hands with well-wishers. Al Blake said the secret to a long and happy marriage is to give each other space.

"Come and go as you want. Just be honest," he said. "If I want to go fishing and she wants to go shopping, that's all right."

The couple has two children and three grandchildren. They have lived in Palm Beach Shores for 23 years.

"It's just a quiet, laid back, little, friendly town," Al Blake said.

Tommy and Claire Knight moved from the hustle and bustle of Philadelphia to the quiet of Palm Beach Shores six years ago. Tommy Knight is a former Mummer, a group of Philadelphians who dress up in feathers and finery on New Year's Day to strut through the center of the city.

The couple keeps a storage shed full of elaborate Mummers costumes and on Saturday, they persuaded about 25 friends to dress up and participate in the Palm Beach Shores parade.

Tommy Knight said he misses marching in the real Mummers parade in Philadelphia, but the couple love living in Florida.

"What's not to like?" he asked. "It's beautiful and we're a block from the ocean."

Not everyone loves a parade. For Chris Brennan of the Philadelphia Daily News, parade stories are the equivalent of root canal. Here is how he handles these assignments:

I hate parade stories. They're interchangeable and entirely predictable. Some reporter roams up and down the crowd, talking to some dad with a kid on his shoulders or some mom pushing a stroller about how much the kids love Santa/ the Easter Bunny/St. Patrick/etc.

I had to cover Philadelphia's Thanksgiving Day Parade one year, so I asked around a few days in advance and learned that one of the key producers had started in the parade years ago as a kid on a float when her dad was a parade volunteer. I set it up that I would shadow her for the day, starting at the ungodly hour of 5 a.m. We zipped around the parade all day in a golf cart, attending to one emergency after another. Then I wrote it up as a Day in the Life.

Protests

While most parades and festivals are fun and easy assignments, protests can be downright stressful, and even scary. During a protest, people's emotions are running high and the issue is usually a serious one. Protesters are often angry and law enforcement officials are on high alert, especially in large cities and after 9/11.

The Arab Spring protests in the Middle East in 2011 were especially dangerous for journalists. Lara Logan of CBS News was assaulted in Egypt. Award-winning news photographers Tim Hetherington and Chris Hondros were shot and killed while covering the uprising in Libya. Other reporters were arrested and beaten.

During the Occupy Wall Street protests in the fall of 2011, many reporters were arrested and taken to jail.

Journalists should strive NOT to get arrested, but if you do, make sure your press pass is visible and you have the number of your newsroom's attorney memorized. International reporters should know how to contact the United States Embassy and what their rights are in that country. One Egyptian-American reporter who was arrested managed to borrow a cell phone shortly after her arrest and post her predicament on Twitter.

A reporter should get close to the protest but try to remain safe at the same time. Use common sense and try to work with a companion journalist.

Protests are news because the stories feature something that is at the heart of most good stories – conflict. One side disagrees with another and expresses it – but in a loud and assertive way.

Here is an excerpt from the New York Daily News from Aug. 30, 2004 when protestors flooded New York City during the Republican Convention. It was written by Corky Siemaszko and more than 30 reporters from the

Daily News contributed to stories about the protests.

The first few paragraphs of that story meld the serious with the silly. The journalists paint the scene of people dressed as dancing Statue of Liberties while others wave signs and scream. But the story makes clear that the crowd was angry. They were "screaming denunciations." Their sheer numbers looked like "a raging sea." And since this was after 9/11, in New York City, the police were out in full force.

7th Ablaze with Anti-Bush Fervor

A raging sea of protesters opposed to President Bush and the Iraq war washed over Seventh Ave. yesterday in the biggest display of dissent at a political convention in U.S. history.

Waving signs and screaming denunciations, the throngs were flanked by cops every step of the way from Union Square to Madison Square Garden. It was the NYPD's largest planned mobilization ever.

The Uncle Sams on stilts and the dancing Statue of Liberty gave the demonstration a carnival-like air. But on the eve of the Republican National Convention, most of the protesters were deadly serious, defiantly anti-Bush, and largely law-abiding.

Bob King is a longtime environmental reporter who is now at Politico. When he was at the Palm Beach Post, he wrote hundreds of stories about the Everglades. Here is one story about a showdown between police and environmentalists:

Some protests are more exciting than others. Sometimes it's just a few dozen people sitting in the audience at a government meeting while wearing the same color T-shirt. Other times you'll see 10 people standing outside an office building while holding up pre-printed signs and reciting some kind of slogan. ("What do we want? Everglades audit," one such protest went a few years ago. "When do we want it? Now!")

But Feb. 18, 2008 was different. That was the day more than 120 environmentalists blockaded the construction site for a natural-gas-burning power plant in western Palm Beach County, Florida, just across the street from the northernmost remnants of the Everglades.

The protest was nonviolent, although it led to 27 arrests and snarled traffic on the county's major east-west highway for five hours. It was also modest in size compared with major demonstrations like the 1963 March on Washington. Still, it taught me several lessons about covering this kind of event:

• Bring water, sunscreen and a hat: First of all, you never know how long one of these events is going to last. The activists, most of them from the radical

movement Earth First!, initially began the morning by marching to the power plant construction site from a nature preserve about a half-mile away. But while that was going on, a separate group of the protesters showed up at the construction site, made it past the modest sheriff's deputy guard detail and blockaded the entrance so that no trucks could enter or leave the property.

The marchers soon joined them, and a bunch of the protesters formed an immovable obstacle by lying on the site's driveway with their arms linked together by PVC pipe. Trucks began backing up onto the main highway, blocking traffic for miles. And the authorities began mobilizing their response – a huge mobile command center, 60 members of the sheriff's "emergency field force," 20 road deputies, 10 corrections officers and about 35 county fire-rescue workers.

The deputies negotiated with the protesters for a while but didn't begin making arrests until more than three hours after the start of the protest. Traffic wasn't back to normal until two hours after that.

I had no hat, no sunscreen and no water for those five hours under the South Florida sun. I was extremely red the next day.

• Have a way to communicate with your home base: I did bring my laptop with a huge spare battery, plus an air card allowing me to get on the Internet, which let me write feeds for the website and email them to my editors. (Nowadays we'd probably have used a BlackBerry or smartphone.) I also recorded audio interviews with the cops and protesters and sent those MP3 files along as well. And my newspaper sent several photographers, who were all smart enough to wear hats.

• Talk to all sides: In this case that included the protesters, one of whom was an aide to a local congressman, along with the cops, the employees at the construction site and nearby rock mine, and the truckers who were all stuck in traffic. Luckily, none of these folks were going anywhere for a while.

• Don't be afraid to stand your ground with the cops: Law enforcement has a job to do, and you absolutely shouldn't do anything that breaks the law, interferes with them or creates a safety hazard. On the other hand, you have a job to do as well – and rights, especially when you're on public right-of-way.

So when the deputies insisted that all journalists had to move to a "media area" more than 10 yards away from where the cops were cutting the PVC pipes and hauling away the protesters, I complied while making the point (more than once) that we needed to be able to see what the authorities were doing. The protesters were making the same point, chanting "Let the media see!"

I also later walked around the entire law enforcement perimeter to get to a "free speech" area and interview activists who had been closer to the action. (I walked along the same public right-of-way that deputies had been telling straggling protesters to use. If it was good enough for them, it was good enough for me.)

• *Follow up: What happened to the people who were arrested? Did they end up with jail time or were the cases dismissed? And what happened to whatever they were protesting about? (In this case, the plant ended up being built.)*

Festivals

Art, music and automobiles. All of these are fodder for festivals. A reporter who spends any time working at a small newspaper, television station or radio station will have to cover a festival.

This is a typical festival story that I wrote for the Palm Beach Post about the annual Street Painting Festival. The twist was that the paintings were done with chalk. And it rained. This was unexpected because Florida was in the middle of a dreadful drought.

To write this story, I drove to the town and spent a while just walking around. I looked at all the drawings and tried to figure out how to describe them. Since I am no artist, I stuck with basic descriptions, such as the black and yellow chalk on the van Gogh chalk copy. The rain was a bad thing for the festival but a good twist for my story, since I was able to watch the artists frantically trying to protect their chalk creations. This provided some action to a story that was quite static in nature, since it was basically just a bunch of people drawing on the street.

Here is the story:

> LAKE WORTH – Even in a drought, rain can sometimes be a pain.
>
> A brief afternoon shower Saturday sent artists at the annual Street Painting Festival running for cover and searching for large sheets of plastic to protect their chalk creations. The festival, which continues today from 10 a.m. to 6 p.m., takes place on Lake Avenue and also features music, food and street performers.
>
> Artists use chalk to create familiar and original scenes on the asphalt. Covered in chalk dust and sprawled on the ground, they drew and daubed with brushes and fingers.
>
> When the rain fell, about 4 p.m., there was a frantic scurrying for cover by the patrons and plastic by the artists.
>
> Two art students from Santaluces High School spread plastic over their picture, then Jessica Villa, 17, and Risto Nylander, 18, lay down on top of it to keep the sheeting from flying away.
>
> The pair, who take Advanced Placement art, copied Vincent van Gogh's painting Starry Night. With black and yellow chalk, they

swirled the colors on the ground into the familiar picture.

Farther down the street, Jeanie Burns held up a transparency of an 1820 painting by a French Romantic painter Anne-Louis Girodet-Trioson. Burns was copying the red and golden hues of Woman in a Turban onto the black street.

Burns is a graphic artist who created the design for the festival's T-shirts. With black chalk all over her legs and arms, she squinted at the transparency and back down again at the unfinished chalk portrait.

The woman looks wistful, her gaze off in the distance. Burns said it was that gaze that led her to choose the portrait.

"I was going through images and I thought it was nice," she said. "I looked at her eyes."

The festival also featured street performers such as Randy Orwig of Loxahatchee. Dressed in black and white, with a beret atop his head, Orwig was the Living Statue. He froze in position as people stood and stared.

Except for one guy, who chose to greet the Living Statue with the salutation from a beer commercial.

"WASSSSSSUUUUUUUP!" the guy bellowed. "Hey, I got him to move his head!"

10 Tips on *Covering Parades and Protests*

- Dress appropriately. If you are covering a protest, dress with safety in mind.

- Capture all the color. These stories are all about sights and sounds.

- Always carry an extra notebook and pencil in case it rains. Pens don't work in the rain on damp notebook paper.

- Look for the unexpected or offbeat, like someone NOT dressed in green.

- Eat a fried Twinkie at the state fair. This is research.

- Always go to the bathroom before you leave the newsroom, unless you want to rely on a smelly portable toilet. And you do not.

- Avoid clichés in your writing

- Get the name of the dog. Especially if it is wearing a silly hat.

- When covering a protest, memorize the phone number of your organization's attorney in case you get arrested.

- If you are overseas, memorize the number of the U.S. Embassy in that country.

In-Class Activity/Homework

Look up information about the 2011 Arab Spring uprising in Tunisia, Egypt, and Libya. Now look up videos of those protests. Imagine that you were a college student in Egypt during the uprisings and wanted to cover the protests for your college newspaper or blog.

Write down the five steps you would take in order to cover the protests, while trying not to compromise your safety.

Journalist Q&A

Lisa L. Colangelo

Where do you work?
Staff Writer at the New York Daily News.

What is your beat?
I work in the Queens Bureau covering local stories as well as citywide and breaking news. I also write a weekly Civil Service column focused on New York City municipal employees.

Where did you go to college and what was your degree?
Queens College at the City University of New York; dual major English Writing and Political Science/ Communications

Did you work on your college newspaper?
Yes, I was assistant news editor, news editor and editor of my college paper.

Did you have any internships? If so, where and what did you do?
I had several internships while I was in college. I worked at the Queens Tribune, a local weekly paper, and covered Queens-based news in 1984. I also had an American Society of Magazine Editors internship (summer 1985) at Gralla Publications writing for Corporate Travel. I worked as an intern at the Columbia Journalism Review (1985) where I wrote, and assisted editors with research and fact-checking. I also interned at WNBC-TV in New York City in 1987. On occasion I would get to go out with a reporter on assignment or watch them edit a story. But most of the time I answered the phone and got the assignment editors food. The one highlight was getting into a taping of "Late Night with David Letterman" because I was a huge fan. The people were nice but since I worked the 4 p.m.-midnight shift I didn't get to do all that much.

When and where was your first journalism job? What is one thing you learned from it?
My first newspaper job was working as a reporter/editor at the Queens Tribune – a weekly paper in Queens where I grew up and went to college. That experience helped me learn the basics of writing and reporting stories on a much different level than I had done at the college paper.

My first daily newspaper job came two years later at the North Jersey Herald & News. That is where I really learned how to cover a beat, handle breaking news and write multiple stories a day. I learned to be persistent and push myself no matter how tough or uncomfortable I found the assignment. I covered towns and I visited them every day even if administrators in the municipal buildings continued to tell me there was nothing going on.

What was the hardest part of your first journalism job?

Learning how to cover a municipal beat even when no one in the town would give you a clue about stories. I went to meetings and made connections and eventually broke through the walls of silence. But there were some really tough days early on. I remember sitting in the parking lot of the shopping centers on Route 46 and trying to gather my thoughts about how to handle certain situations. It was grueling but I learned so much. Eventually I moved onto larger beats and towns and school districts where there were endless stories and not enough time to do them all.

Many beginning journalists get very nervous about their first assignments. Did you get nervous and how did you cope?

Of course. That's natural and anyone who tells you otherwise is full of it. Just do as much research in advance as possible before you cover a meeting or start a new beat. Hopefully more seasoned reporters at the paper will give you advice and support. You might get lucky and even find helpful reporters from other news outlets at the scene – but don't count on it. Just gather your thoughts and try to remember what you have to do.

What is the worst part about being a journalist?

I won't say low pay and long hours because that's crap. No one should get into this business for money or normal hours. You need the passion and the drive. But it always kind of stinks when you have to knock on the door and ask someone about a loved one who was killed, or is accused of killing someone. It's really nerve wracking to be on a busy scene and worry that a competitor is getting a witness or an important source that you don't have.

What is the best part?

Being able to write about and experience things that you find fun and interesting on a regular basis. You also have the chance to highlight good deeds and interesting people and really make a difference in their lives. And perhaps most importantly you can step in and help someone who is being wronged or uncover some misuse of public funds or other dastardly deed. In some places we are the only people closely watching what is going on.

What advice would you give to a journalism major?

Work at your college newspaper or other media outlet. Find internships paid or unpaid that will give you valuable experience and help build your resume. Make connections and stay in touch with people.

Chapter 8
Profiles

Courtesy of Steve Lubetkin

Profiles are among my favorite stories to write and that is true for many journalists, especially feature writers. A profile can reveal a person's thoughts, dreams and flaws. A profile can be a window into someone's soul or just a quirky slice of life.

Profiles give us an insight into high-profile people, such as politicians, athletes and celebrities. They shine light on those who might not normally get much recognition, such as ministers, teachers and police officers. When we read profiles of parents, professionals and pet lovers, we relate to them and see that we are often more alike than different.

Writing profiles is a wonderful form of journalism because the style can take many different tones: serious, snarky or humorous, to name a few. While the focus should remain on the profile subject, a reporter's personality can be infused into the article and shape it a bit.

Profiles can use elements of fiction writing, such as flashbacks and foreshadowing. But remember – just because the article uses ELEMENTS of fiction writing, doesn't mean the article itself can BE fiction. You must check out every fact in the story and print them only if they are true. Profiles are a form of journalism and they are grounded in reality.

Dialogue can be very effective in a profile. So can ordinary people in extraordinary situations.

Read this Times-Picayune profile of a woman named Momma D, who helped out her neighbors in New Orleans in the aftermath of Hurricane Katrina. The reporter, Trymaine D. Lee, gets the cadence of the woman's voice and listens for the important dialogue. He uses the dialogue to move the story along.

Diane "Momma D" Frenchcoat rises early each morning and pushes a cart of food and supplies through the sludge-spoiled streets of Treme and the 7th Ward.

She delivers food and hope for the hungry. She serves the delusional and dejected, the junkies and the flood survivors who have remained in the city despite its mass evacuation.

Each day, she pushes her cart up and down (the streets), calling to those too ill or too old or too stubborn to leave the neighborhoods that they've loved for so long.

"You need something to eat?" Frenchcoat yelled to a skinny, shirtless man perched in a second-floor window of a home on Esplanade near Treme Street, earlier this week. "You hungry? You want some food?"

The man peered down from his post to the mud-crusted block

below and responded with silence.

"You need some food, baby?" Frenchcoat hollered again.

The man stood there for a moment then vanished into the darkness.

"So many of them are scared to come out of their homes. But they're hungry, I know they are. So, I just come by every day and let them get used to my voice and hope they come out."

Notice that Lee uses a list of "threes." He describes how Momma D pushes her cart along the streets, calling out to those "too ill or too old or too stubborn." Lists work best in threes – there is a rhythm to the writing and reading of them.

Lee said he tries to "tap into who the subject really is." He does that through details of time and place, such as the "sludge-covered streets" of New Orleans.

Here is something that always seems to startle my students: You do not have to like the profile subject in order to write about him or her. In fact, sometimes it works against reporters if they like their profile subjects – it can make it harder to be fair and accurate.

But people are interesting, warts and all. Racists, tyrants and just-plain jerks can all make good profile subjects. I have interviewed Ku Klux Klan members, criminals and a good share of morons. They can all make good copy.

Here is the beginning of a profile I wrote about an oddball, elderly man in Lake County, FL and his love of lawsuits. It appeared in the Orlando Sentinel:

MOUNT DORA – Ed Brennan, retiree, is spending his golden years on three things: collecting machine guns, filing lawsuits and preventing police from masturbating in their patrol cars.

Sometimes, all three are connected – at least to Brennan, a 73-year-old decorated World War II veteran and retired auto body shop owner who glories in irritating people.

He thinks government is a giant conspiracy, big business is crooked and most people are out to get him. He believes the quickest way to right a wrong is to file a lawsuit.

If the Eustis cops give him a ticket, Brennan sues. The Wal-Mart annoys him; he sues. He once sued his children while settling a divorce with his former wife. His suits get thrown out, but not before defendants – often the taxpayers – get socked with legal fees.

Brennan, on the other hand, has almost nothing invested – he pecks out the documents with two fingers on his typewriter.

"You might think I'm a nut," Brennan said in an interview last week. "But I don't care."

I let my humor come through a bit in the profile of Brennan, because I got the sense that he simply enjoyed being a bit of a pain. I also made him promise not to sue ME if I wrote an article in the newspaper about him.

The path of Brennan's life played out along a series of "Turning Points," such as his marriage and then his divorce. Pay attention to the Turning Points in the life of your profile subject. They are those moments – some big and some small – that shape a person's life. Birth, death and divorce are some obvious ones. So is losing a job, finding a wife or becoming ill.

People's lives move from Point A to Point B because of Turning Points. Most of us don't even realize at the time the significance certain conversations and events will have in our lives in the future.

It doesn't matter how old a person is, either. The Turning Points never stop coming.

Check out this excerpt from a profile of a Texas man who learned to read when he was 98 years old. Reporter Larry Bingham was working at the Fort Worth Star-Telegram when he met George Dawson and heard his story. Here is the article, which was printed in the Fort Worth Star-Telegram and later reprinted in Reader's Digest. The story also led to an invitation for Dawson to appear on the Oprah Winfrey show.

The 99-year-old Man Who Learned to Read
Fort Worth Star-Telegram

January 19, 1998

By Larry Bingham

DALLAS – The old man who could not read lives alone in a house that is small and square and in a part of the city some people call the ghetto.

George Dawson, the grandson of a slave, was born in a three-room log cabin in Marshall, on Jan. 18, 1898. He was 8 when he had his first job, feeding hogs and cattle. He was 12 when his daddy rented him out to a white man.

His four brothers and sisters learned to read at a school "for colored children." He was the oldest. He didn't get to go to school because he had to work.

He married in 1926 and was a father in 1927. He chopped wood, worked in a sawmill and built levees with the aid of a mule. He laid ties for some of the first railroads in East Texas. He swept floors, cleaned for white people, and for most of his working life – 25 years – ran the machines that pasteurized milk at Oak Farms Dairy, where he lost a one-time chance at a promotion because the boss asked him to sign his name and he marked an X instead.

The old man got by without reading for 98 years. He trusted the people who paid his wages, had no need for books or bank accounts, and his wife read the bills.

He married twice, was widowed twice, and raised seven children. All of them learned to read and write at Lincoln High School, a few blocks from his house. "I seen to 'em, every one. I didn't get to go to school, so I seen to them."

The old man got by until 1996, when a young man knocked on his door and said he was recruiting people for the Adult Basic Education classes at the old high school.

"I've been alone for 10 years," the old man told him. "I'm tired of fishing. It's time to learn to read."

He waited outside Classroom 103, and the teacher looked at him: He stood barely 5 feet tall. His skin was wrinkled, his hair was white. His blue eyes said he was serious.

You ever go to school?

Not a day.

Not a day?

Never had a chance.

Know the alphabet?

No, son.

The teacher began with six letters, but the old man interrupted.

"No, son. I want to see all of them. I want to put 'em together."

The old man learned his ABCs in a day and a half. The teacher moved on to phonics, breaking words into pieces and sounding out the parts.

"No, son. I want to say something that makes sense."

From 9 a.m. to 1 p.m., every Monday through Friday, except for the three days he missed class to go to funerals, the old man sat in the same seat on the second row. On the bulletin board behind him, the laminated faces of Ella Fitzgerald, Rosa Parks, Alex Hailey, Jesse Jackson, Martin Luther King Jr., Coretta Scott King, Thurgood

Marshall, Nelson Mandela, Desmond Tutu and Booker T. Washington watched over him.

He mastered print and moved into cursive. The first few times he wrote his name, he left a space between the last "g" and the "e" on George. He never liked the lowercase letters "f," "j" and "q."

"Them three letters, you got to put your mind on what you're doing," he said.

At the end of the first month, he could write his name. After almost two years, he can read on a third-grade level.

He likes to read at a folding card table that he keeps beside a couch that is covered with a sheet, beside a coffee table covered with a towel, in a living room so close to the street he can hear people walking by.

Now that he can, he reads the Scriptures aloud at Holiness Church of God if they ask him. At home, he reads Ephesians from an old Bible that cost him $23 who-knows-how-many years ago in Mississippi.

He needs glasses but won't wear them. The teacher told him he needs a hearing aid, but he told the teacher, "Talk a little louder, son."

For the first time in a century, he carries a brown book bag, writes with a No. 2 pencil and erases what is not good enough for him.

"I always thought I could drive a spike as good as any man. I cook as good as any woman I ever met. ...

"I'd go everywhere and see people read. I'd go places and streets I didn't know where I was. I just figured if everybody else can learn to read, I could too."

His 100th birthday is Sunday, but his teachers and fellow students at Lincoln Instructional Center threw him a party on Friday. It was supposed to be a surprise, but he overheard them talking about it.

When he opens his cards, he will read every word. Because he can.

Here is a Q&A I had with Bingham:

Q. How did you find George Dawson?

I was watching TV news one night after I had recently moved from North Carolina to Texas. I was bored and waiting for my family to come. The TV show featured a segment on an adult reading center. They mentioned the 100-year-old man as one of their students. I needed a story and the journey of how a man learns to read at 99 was an easy story to see.

Q. Did you have any problems in dealing with an elderly profile subject?

No problems, really. He was hard of hearing and kept his house in Dallas sauna hot but otherwise he required no special treatment other than the same things all our subjects need of us: attention and patience.

Q. How did you get such good details – the letters he didn't like to write, such as a lower case "q" and "j?"

From interviewing his teacher. I always think of something reporter Anne Hull once said (she's at the Washington Post now) about finding "rabbis" for our stories. What I took that to mean was to seek people who could tell you what the protagonist of the story might not. Someone to explain things. In this case, the mechanics of how the learning went.

Q. How did you structure the story?

I very much wanted the syntax and diction of the story to reveal character and reflect the "story"-like nature of that situation. Here was someone learning to read, so the situation could be told naturally with simple language, short sentences, and in a fairly straight-forward, chronological narrative. I knew I could borrow those elements from children's books. It helped, by the way, that my boys were young at that time, and I had at my fingertips plenty of examples of how simple stories operated.

That archetype is one reason I used the words "the old man" so often. I opened with a scene setter in the present time that would establish the scenario and tell the readers what to expect, that this was going to be a story about how an old man learned to read. Then I rewound the narrative tape and told the story from beginning to end, coming back to the present-time situation and his 100th birthday party and his ability to read, for the first time, his birthday cards.

Here is another profile by Bingham. This story, from The (Baltimore) Sun, is about a dedicated teenager named Bobby Stiles, who lives on a farm in Maryland. Stiles' father became ill with cancer. Bingham chronicled the teen's struggle to keep the family farm going while also trying to pursue a college education. The story won first place in its category for the American Association of Sunday and Feature Editors.

The following is an excerpt:

On the day he was supposed to leave the farm and go to college, Bobby's mother came into his room at 4 a.m. and turned on the light.

Bobby knew what the white glare meant. It was a bugle call, his mother's way of saying something bad had happened, she needed help, time for the new man of the house to get up.

He didn't wash his face or mess with his hair or even look at himself in the mirror. Bobby Stiles wasn't that kind of teenager. He kept his hair stubble-short, and he owned only one nice pair of tennis shoes for the nights he drove into town to hang out with friends. He saved his money for a gleaming Dodge Ram and for college.

Bobby found his work shoes by the door, where he left them when he came in from the milking parlor. They were big shoes, bigger than his father's, and like all the pairs parked around the door mat, they smelled of manure. He stepped into them without a second thought.

Notice the details: his hair is kept "stubble-short." He is saving money for a Dodge Ram. His shoes smell like manure. This description gives the reader an accurate feel for Bobby Stiles. He is clearly a farm boy. He is not a fussy or glamorous person.

And the story revolves around a very important Turning Point in Stiles' life: the illness of his father.

10 Tips on *Writing Profiles*

- You MUST include the person's full name, age, marital status, birthplace, family, job and hobbies.

- What does the person look and sound like? Tall, short, stocky, lean?

- Listen first, ask questions later. Pay attention to more than what the person is saying. Observe. What is on the person's desk? The walls? The color of nail polish?

- Don't be afraid of silence. Don't feel compelled to cram every single moment with questions.

- State the ground rules up front. Is everything on the record? Is a publicist permitted in the room? If you're using a tape recorder, tell the subject.

- Know how to deal with subjects who want to veer off subject. You know the type – people who take 15 minutes to answer a thirty-second question, and by the end of the interview have bored you to tears. An interview is like a river and YOU are steering the boat, not the interview subject.

- The corollary to the above rule is know when to throw your question list out the window and go with the story you weren't expecting. Good editors – and good reporters – know that they have to be flexible.

- Spend as much time as possible with the person. Go to the person's job, meet his/her family. Follow the person around till he/she forgets you are there.

- Conduct the interview in person. Phone interviews and e-mail interviews rarely work very well in profiles and are not recommended except under tight deadlines.

- Catch the visual rhythm. So much is going on. Pay close attention to everything around the person. Before asking your first question, take a visual survey. All of those details will make for great clay to slap onto the sculpture that your story will become.

In-Class Activity/Homework

• What "Turning Points" have you experienced in your own life? (i.e. Births, deaths, marriage, divorce, new school, new relationship, break ups, jobs, getting fired, travel, awards)

• How did those "Turning Points" affect you?

• Divide up in class into groups of two. Chat with your classmate. What does that person look like? (Hair, clothes, shoes, jewelry) What does the person sound like? Describe.

Journalist Q&A

Mary Ellen Flannery

Where do you work?
National Education Association

What is your Job Title?
Editor, NEA Office of Higher Education

Where did you go to college and what was your degree?
Georgetown, B.A., English; Northwestern, M.A., Journalism.

Did you have any internships? If so, where and what did you do?

When I was at journalism school, I took the summer off to intern at the South Bend Tribune in Indiana. I worked for the local news editor and mostly I wrote about county fairs. Lots and lots of county fairs! They're a big deal in Indiana. So I covered the chicken fly-off, the rocket launch contest, the 4-H dress design competition ... I tried to find the "unwritten" county fair story – like the guy running the no-win carnival game who showed me his bullet scars and said he enjoyed travel.

When and where was your first journalism job? What is one thing you learned from it?

I worked in the Port St. Lucie bureau of the Stuart News in Florida. I covered schools – everything from Head Start to the local, very ambitious community college. Oh, I learned a lot of things!

One, do not be afraid to knock on doors. Most people are surprisingly nice to a stranger on their step, especially a young, reasonably friendly one.

Two, some people lie. It's true! Don't believe everything you hear, especially if you hear it from a man in a suit. It was shocking when I realized the school superintendent was actually dissembling to my face.

Three, it's always a good idea to have friendly relations with the official spokespeople that you're covering. In my first job, my relationship with the school district's public information officer deteriorated to the point where I had to file a complaint with the state attorney's office, alleging that she had been violating state law by withholding public records from me. (The state attorney ordered the release of the documents.)

But, in retrospect, I think I went in there with my hair on fire, got her back up, and created a situation where nobody could possibly win. In future relationships with persons of interest, I tried to walk a finer line. We'd meet for coffee. I'd say things like, "Don't make me file a records request for this. Neither of us need the stress, honey."

But also keep this in mind: You are rarely going to get good stories from a public spokesman. That's not their job. If you want information that nobody else has, you need to cultivate the people who rarely get heard. In my first job, I got great stories from a school bus mechanic who led a support staff union that nobody paid attention to, and also a school district IT guy who I met at a bar.

What was the hardest part of your first journalism job?

Managing time. There were plenty of days when I worked 12 hours. I'm pretty sure it shouldn't have taken so long to file two 12-inch stories!

Many beginning journalists get very nervous about their first assignments. Did you get nervous and how did you cope?

I worked in a very competitive news environment in my first job – three daily newspapers were covering the same small community. It was crazy. (And it's not true anymore. Since then, two of those papers have merged and the third pulled out of that market.) Every morning, I'd come into the newsroom and look at the competition and kill myself over whatever I had missed.

Eventually, the oldest reporter in the room – a very kind Korean War vet named Joe – took me out to the local BBQ place and was like, "Listen, you're doing a fine job. Quit beating yourself up." So my first piece of advice is – find a mentor. Look for somebody who knows their way around a beat and a story, and just say, "Hey, can I buy you a coffee? I'm pretty sure I'm doing a wicked poor job here and I'd really like your advice." (Old reporters are suckers for anybody who recognizes their talents. Nobody would say no.)

Second, do your own thing. I remember actually going into the bureau's bathroom to cry because the competition had a story about the superintendent's secretary's retirement. Oh my God! Who cares? Not one of their readers even knew that woman.

In retrospect, I was wasting my time – and making myself red and puffy for nothing -- trying to figure out what the competition was doing. Figure out what kind of story you do best. Figure out what kind of story your readers actually respond to. Do that instead.

What is the worst part about being a journalist?

I think your world can get a little small. You start hanging out with journalists only. You start dating journalists, drinking with journalists, talking about stories and newsroom personalities all the time. This is not healthy. (It's also not economically sound. Eventually, if you marry another journalist, you'll both be at the whims of the same market. It's better for your financial security to diversify your income stream!)

What is the best part?

When I was a kid, my father took me to work with him a couple of times a year. He was a building inspector – he spent 30 minutes in the office in the morning and 30 minutes in the afternoon. In between, he drove around to building sites and met his pals for coffee. I decided then that he had exactly the kind of job I wanted. As a journalist, you do not have to sit in an office all day. (And if you're a good reporter, you will not sit in an office all day.)

You'll get paid to talk to people who have interesting things to say. And, this is not a cliché, you will do something good for the world you live in. You will help kids stay healthy. You will keep bad drivers off the road. You will make sure your parents have a secure retirement. You will save natural resources. You will afflict the comfortable and comfort the afflicted. (I didn't write that line. I think Mencken did.) You will have the ability and the means to actually save lives.

What advice would you give to a beginning journalist?

Start reading good journalism. You don't have to buy the newspaper – although that would be nice! But you need to read it. And start paying attention to the things you like to read. Ask yourself why you like it. Did it have a great lede? Did the quotes grab your attention? Pay attention to what you don't like, too.

What would you tell yourself at the beginning of your career, if you could go back in time?

I don't think you could have told the 22-year-old me to wear more appropriate clothes but I wonder if that might have helped in some situations. I look at kids today (do I sound old?) and think, "I wouldn't trust you with a secret! I think it would leak out your cleavage."

Somebody once told me that you want to dress like the people you cover – and I think that's a good idea. If you're hanging out in the courtroom with lawyers, put on a tie. If you're hanging out with teachers, grab your Dansko clogs, etc.

Chapter 9
Children and Families

Courtesy of Thomas Parmalee

Almost anyone can cover the cops beat, but it takes skill and finesse to write about children and families issues.

Children and families journalism may not leap to the forefront of beginning journalists' minds, but the topics are everywhere: dirty day care centers, teens and video games, poverty in the inner city and suburbs.

Everyone was a child once and belongs to a family. No longer are these topics relegated to the antiquated "women's pages" of the newspaper. The topics range from child abuse to juvenile crime, to health, to education issues. They are challenging, intense and rewarding stories to report and write.

Journalists who write about these issues are feature writers, investigative reporters and hard news journalists. These stories attract readers, they win awards and more importantly – they matter. These stories can also break your heart.

However, children and families stories do not always get the attention they need from editors or the play they deserve in newspapers, magazines and television. Some of these stories are still (wrongly) perceived as "soft" and only catch the attention of editors and bosses when violence occurs, such as a school shooting or the death of a foster child.

This point of view is a fallacy. Issues like over-crowded schools, the rates of child asthma and inept social workers are affecting society right now and will continue to in the future. These topics are wide open for reporters who like to scratch below the surface and determine what is really going on, and not just continue to reprint conventional wisdom or the status quo.

Like many reporters, I set out to be a features writer and wound up as a news reporter with an eye for detail and characters. I stumbled into children and families journalism because of various stories I was covering, such as an over-crowded juvenile detention center or the increase in the number of grade-schoolers being medicated for attention deficit disorder.

In 1999, I was lucky enough to be the recipient of the Casey Journalism Fellowship in children and families reporting when I was at the University of Maryland earning my master's degree in journalism. That fellowship helped shape me as a journalist, educator and person.

By writing this chapter, I am spreading the word about children and families reporting. I hope this chapter spurs some ideas for stories and the need to report them.

The trouble is, reporters covering these stories must often battle with editors to get them the "play" they deserve. Editors often (wrongly) assume that the stories take too much time, are too complicated or are too depressing.

Sometimes they are. But they still need to be told and NOT just in a time of crisis.

Here are some story ideas for the children and families beat:

- Rankings of day care centers in your area. Which ones are dirty and dangerous?

- The local child welfare system: Are there enough foster families? Did child welfare workers fail to remove an abused child from a home? What happens to foster children when they turn 18?

- What are the juvenile crime trends in your area?

- A week in juvenile court. Access to juvenile courts varies from state to state. Some juvenile courts are closed to the press entirely; some allow the press only with a judge's order while others (such as Florida) are completely open.

- Teens and technology. How teenagers communicate, with social networking, instant messages and text messages

- Children's health issues, such as attention deficit disorder, autism and the controversy over vaccines.

- Are today's kindergartners smarter than they were 20 years ago?

- The face of the family is changing. The model of the two-parent (man/woman) family still remains but many other forms of family now exist, such as lesbian parents, single parents and parents who never marry.

- More female parents work than ever before. What are the issues of mothers who work outside the home and their children?

In 2002, the Casey Journalism Center on Children and Families commissioned a study of news content over a three-month period. The study found that 90 percent of print and television stories about children were mostly focused on crime and violence, such as child abuse deaths.

I experienced that myself as a reporter. The trick is to build on the momentum from those high-profile stories, like child abuse deaths and juvenile crime, and turn them into long-term beats and projects. It can be done.

Candy J. Cooper wrote about the struggle of children and families reporters in an article in the Fall 2005 issue of The Children's Beat, the newsletter of the Casey Journalism Center at the University of Maryland.

"And children's stories take time – if reporters seek more than an adult view, or an adult view conveyed through a child's mouth," Cooper wrote. "Finding authentic children's voices outside the realm of an institution requires an extra layer of reporting. Reporters must locate articulate kids, cultivate their trust and catch them between school dismissal and whatever happens afterward."

In Florida, I covered the story of a little six-year-old girl named Kayla McKean who disappeared from outside her family's apartment on Thanksgiving Day 1998. The little girl's mother sent her to live with her father – even though he had not spent much time with Kayla since she had been born.

Here is an excerpt of the story I wrote for the Orlando Sentinel a day or so after she disappeared while volunteers and police officers searched for her, thinking she had been kidnapped.

CLERMONT – The timid little blonde playing by herself on the worn-out playground caught the eye of Clermont Police Officer Norris Fails many times.

Fails knew the first-grader by sight – barely 4 feet tall and usually alone on the beat-up swings. He always waved at her, but she would look away. She never waved back.

Now, Fails is out to find her. Six-year-old Kayla McKean disappeared Thanksgiving Day outside the apartments at 804 Grand Highway where she lives with her father and stepmother.

Fails was the first officer to arrive, and he didn't need much of a description before he identified her: the painfully shy one.

Kayla went out to play about 9:30 a.m. Thursday and she was gone an hour later.

Her father, Richard Adams, and his wife, Marcie, searched until noon before they sought help.

"They should have called us earlier," Fails said. "The more I think about it, the more I think we would have found her by now. The longer the time goes by, the worse it looks."

The girl's mother, however, said she thinks her "stubborn" little daughter will be found. Elizabeth McKean's voice quavered and her eyes brimmed with tears as she answered questions about the youngster who recently lost a front tooth and loves to play in the park.

The story Kayla's father told was a lie, of course. She hadn't disappeared. He beat her till she bled to death internally, then he made his wife help him haul the little girl's body away and dump her in the woods. Richard Adams was convicted of murder and is serving a life sentence in a Florida prison.

Kayla's death might have been prevented. At least three calls were made to a child abuse hotline about Kayla by concerned citizens. Several different social workers saw Kayla on different occasions but believed her father's lies about her injuries, such as she "fell off a bike" or a "dog stepped on her face."

Here is an excerpt from a story I wrote about the failure of the social workers to protect Kayla from her abusive father.

Social workers who were supposed to protect Kayla McKean shrugged off glaring signs that the 6-year-old Lake County girl was being abused, a report by the state's child welfare agency says.

Without serious scrutiny, the workers accepted stories from Kayla's father and stepmother about why they had to tie the first-grader up to spank her, smeared makeup on her black eyes and forced her to pull weeds and do jumping jacks as punishment.

Those handling Kayla's case at two child welfare agencies were so disturbingly disorganized that nobody had a complete picture of the girl's torment, according to the Department of Children & Families report released Tuesday.

These stories are heart-breaking and depressing and I wrote about 60 of them on the Kayla McKean case over a 12-month period. But all the newspaper, radio and television coverage of Kayla's death had an impact. The coverage led to increased awareness of child abuse and the overloaded child welfare system in Florida. There were major shake-ups in the Department of Children and Families in Florida and "Kayla's Law" was passed to try and prevent future child abuse deaths.

No law can protect all children, however, so reporters covering the child welfare system in their city or state may one day have to write one of these sad stories. Because they need to be told.

Susan K. Livio is an award-winning reporter for the *Star-Ledger* of Newark, NJ. She is based at the statehouse bureau and focuses on social welfare and health issues. Many of her stories deal with children and families issues. Here is a Q&A with Livio:

Q. Why is it important for reporters to cover children and families issues?

So few people in journalism like to tell these stories because they are messy and emotional, with fragile characters caught up in complicated bureaucracies. But this work can really help people – whether through a changed law or additional government funding, or just educating the public on something it needs to understand.

Q. Where can reporters look for children and families topics?

Mine documents. Every year, government and non-profit agencies produce reports or apply for grants and contained therein are data that can offer many ideas. An example: food banks must record who uses their services in order to apply for money. Such a report could tell you where the hidden pockets of poverty exist, even within seemingly well-to-do counties. The state attorney general produces an annual report on civil lawsuit payouts, and usually there are several involving foster children who suffered abuse while under the state's care.

Breaking news – particularly the heart-wrenching family tragedy sort like domestic violence, fatal fires or murders – oozes ideas. I wrote a series on domestic violence after a woman died within days of getting a restraining order against her ex-boyfriend. Two fatalities at psychiatric hospitals led to larger stories on how little treatment and supervision goes on inside these facilities. Following up six months, 12 months, five years after a significant law passes, like welfare reform, offers a window into how people are affected.

Attend a ground-breaking or a fund-raiser for a non-profit like a homeless shelter (reporters get bombarded by these requests all the time) and ask to spend some time observing the program in action. Write a feature story. These contacts you make in "good times" will remember you. Social media like Twitter and Facebook and narrowly-targeted Google alerts can keep you up-to-date on how these issues are covered in other states.

Once you start writing, the stories will find you.

Q. What story have you written of which you are most proud?

Hard to say. At the end of the year, we've done a story recounting the details of every child who died from abuse and neglect in the prior 12 months, and it felt worthwhile documenting who these kids were and what happened to them. Another reporter and I wrote a series about people living in state institutions for people with developmental disabilities. Before its publication but as soon as state officials understood what our data and sources told us, millions of dollars were made available for hiring people and improving the facilities. The reader response was encouraging too – lots of people grateful that we gave so much attention to an overlooked issue and almost just as many who criticized us for sensationalizing, in their opinion, the problems in the institutions. They feared the institutions would close.

Q. What frustrates you about writing children and families' stories?

It's hard to get editors interested in a story unless there is a crisis attached. This attitude can limit subject matter, compromise depth, and reduce coverage to reactionary blather.

It's discouraging, too, that so much of the reader feedback comes from people who want you to help them, like a social worker or a lawyer would.

People have a romanticized idea of journalists – that one will help save them personally because they cannot afford an attorney or have no faith in the courts. It's very hard to find the truth when so much of this subject matter is protected by confidentiality laws.

The work can be emotionally exhausting. Sources need careful attention. They need to understand how going public may negatively affect them, and in their zeal to tell their story sometimes they are not good judges of how something will play out. Child issues reporters need to be careful and protect some of these people from themselves. Letting someone confess how they conceal welfare fraud (by picking up some side work and not reporting the income for instance) could have some painful consequences, even if it's true that most people can't survive on the paltry public assistance benefits the government provides.

Livio was one of the reporters in 2003 who covered the tale of four adopted boys found starving to death in their home in Collingswood, NJ. The boys were found malnourished and growth-stunted after one of them, 19-year-old Bruce, went rummaging in his neighbor's trash can because he was so hungry. The boys had been foster children and were adopted by a family who apparently fed their biological children and limited the food of the adopted children. The state Department of Youth and Family Services came under fire for missing the signs of neglect in the children. The boys were removed from the abusive home, the adoptive parents were arrested and lawsuits and bureaucratic shake-ups were the result.

A caveat: Anytime a reporter writes about the child welfare system, a flood of phone calls from parents will soon follow. Many want the reporter to be their own personal investigator to probe into their perceived injustices. Other calls are from foster parents understandably frustrated with the bureaucracy of the child welfare agency.

Reporters who cover children and families issues need to develop a system to respond to these calls, or else most of their days will be shot. One tip is to create a file of callers and sort them by complaint. Another is to set a time limit to stay on the phone with these callers and stick to it. A reporter might get 100 calls on the topic and one tip turns out to be valid and breaks open a story. But reporters need to set limits for those other 99 phone calls or else they will never get any work done.

Stories about children can often raise ethical issues. For one thing, it is against the law in many states to print the name of children charged in juvenile court. Even if it is legal, media organizations often have ethics codes in which they set a minimum age in which juveniles can be named or set boundaries according to the crime. Journalists should find out what those ethics codes are in their newsrooms and how they pertain to children.

In Florida, for example, juvenile court hearings are open to the press, but juvenile court records are not. Just because the names are public, however, does not mean that reporters should automatically print the names of the children involved, for instance if they are younger than 13 or if their crime is a misdemeanor. The concept of juvenile court was created in 1899 primarily to give children a chance at rehabilitation instead of punishment.

In the past decade, there has been a trend towards openness in the juvenile courts. My opinion is that any system can be improved by having the "sunshine" of the press shined upon it. But just because the information is available doesn't mean journalists should automatically print all the information when children are involved. Such issues, at the very least, require discussions with editors.

Interviewing children requires extra care. Most schools now require signed release forms from parents before children are allowed to be quoted by reporters or photographed by the media. Find out what the requirements are if you plan to do a story on school grounds.

It is generally unethical to interview children without their parents. This falls under the tenet of "Minimize Harm" in the Society of Professional Journalists' Code of Ethics.

"Minimize Harm" states: *Ethical journalists treat sources, subjects and colleagues as human beings deserving of respect.*

Journalists should: Show compassion for those who may be affected adversely by news coverage. Use special sensitivity when dealing with children and inexperienced sources or subjects.

One of the best resources on this topic is the Journalism Center on Children and Families at the University of Maryland. The center is a non-partisan, nonprofit resource center for journalists who cover these topics. The center inspires and recognizes journalists, helps guide coverage and presents regional and national conferences.

Their website is *journalismcenter.org.*

10 Tips on *Covering Children and Families*

- These stories need to be told. Tell them, even if your editors don't act enthused at first. Show them that readers want to know more about children and families issues.

- Stories about child welfare and juvenile justice often unleash a torrent of reader phone calls and e-mails. Create a system to respond to the reader feedback and stick to it. Don't get sucked into a reader's desire for you to become their personal investigative reporter.

- When interviewing children, show compassion and sensitivity. It is best to interview a child when his or her parents are present or permission has been given.

- Figure out the laws pertaining to juvenile court in your state. If the press is allowed to sit in on juvenile court cases, do so. If not, try to convince a judge to let you in to shine more light on the complicated court process.

- Just because some details about juvenile court cases may be public, it doesn't mean media organizations need to reveal them all.

- These stories can sometimes be sad and draining. If you feel you are getting burned out on the beat, ask your editor to let you report on some other kinds of stories for a bit to get a change of pace.

- Learn to love documents, especially reports. Sure, they can seem boring on the surface, but a dense document about the teen pregnancy rate in your town could lead to an insightful look at a societal issue.

- Look for quirky trends, like the "must-have" latest gadget for new moms.

- Consider your own life. If you are a working parent or were a latchkey child, think about the issues that affect you day-to-day and use them as fodder for story ideas.

- Don't stereotype. Open up your mind to people very different from you.

In-Class Activity/Homework

1. Go to the website for the FBI and look up the most recent Uniform Crime Report for your state. Look at the statistics for those arrested who are under 18 years of age. Is juvenile crime up or down in your state? What are the offenses committed most often by juveniles?

2. Go to the website for the child welfare agency in your state (In New Jersey, it is DYFS). Find statistics about child abuse deaths from the past few years. How many deaths were there? Is the number increasing or decreasing?

Journalist Q&A

Courtesy of Drew Brown

Dianna Cahn

Where did you work?
Stars and Stripes
The Sun Sentinel
The Times Herald-Record
CNN International
The Associated Press

What were your beats and job titles?
Afghanistan correspondent, General
Assignment, Metro reporter, Producer and writer, East Africa reporter, and
Jerusalem reporter

Where did you go to college and what was your degree?
Pratt Institute, Bachelor of Architecture

Did you work on your college newspaper or online news website?
No

Did you have any internships? If so, where and what did you do?
No

When and where was your first journalism job? What is one thing you learned from it?
My first job in journalism was as a translator for the Los Angeles Times correspondent in Jerusalem. When I started, I had no idea what he was looking for and I simply translated articles and struggled with the fast-speaking radio news. Then, a new correspondent came in and made clear what he was looking for. Soon, he took me out on stories where he needed language translation and I watched him and learned.

In the fast-paced news environment of Israeli-Palestinian relations in the early 1990s, there was little time to stop. I learned how to cover a story, ask tough questions, understand the ins and outs of tense politics and learned how humor, analysis and familiarity are all important aspects of telling a good story.

I soon got a part time-job working for United Press International in Jerusalem and then The Associated Press a year after that. By then, the

Israeli-Palestinian peace process was in full form and emotions were high. Palestinians celebrated newfound freedoms and Israelis were divided.

The most powerful lesson I learned was the day Israeli Prime Minister Yitzhak Rabin was assassinated by a nationalist Israeli opposed to giving up the land for peace. Rabin was shot outside a peace rally in Tel Aviv and as the news spread, young people lit candles and formed vigil circles outside the hospital and in the streets.

I was eager to get comment for my newspaper and asked a lot of questions, but people were grieving. I got a few nasty looks and I realized I had to back off, watch the story unfold, allow it to happen.

There are times for questions and times to simply observe.

What was the hardest part of your first journalism job?

The hardest part was dealing with prejudices and preconceived notions that come along with people in the Middle East. Passions and tensions are extreme and intense and labels are easily doled out. To be a good journalist, you often have to take heat from all sides. As the saying goes: If all sides are attacking you, you are doing something right.

Many beginning journalists get very nervous about their first assignments. Did you get nervous and how did you cope?

My first big story was the appeals trial in Jerusalem of a man who'd been convicted of Nazi war crimes. I covered it for my boss at the Los Angeles Times and came back and reported to him everything I saw and heard. I was so excited and when I got home that night, I felt ill.

The next day, I told my boss that I went to bed with flu-like symptoms that night and he laughed. "It's just the adrenaline," he said.

A few months later, there was a huge massacre of Palestinians by an Israeli settler at the holiest site in disputed ancient city of Hebron. The story broke as I was leaving for work that morning. I spent the next three hours never leaving my bedroom, just listening to the radio and television interviews and reports and filing to my boss.

Finally, I got to the office later in the afternoon. He went to Hebron and left me to man the media and gather contacts. I fed him information for 12 hours, then he sat down to write. The next morning, every quote I'd highlighted for him was in the story. He'd taught me well.

What is the worst part about being a journalist?

Until a few years ago, I would have said the money. We have to be the smartest and toughest and quickest and most curious people in the room and often, we get paid the least.

But the sad reality today is that I'd have to say the state of our profession. There is less value for true journalism these days, in a large part due to corporate control of the media and a poor profit showing for news enterprises. That, coupled with the fact that a broad swath of the public believes the worst hype about journalists – that we are scheming, underhanded vultures out only for our own gain – has sent the industry into a tailspin.

What is the best part?

I love being on the front lines of history, of events. I love being able to witness first-hand what other people will read about with fascination. And on the occasion where my work actual exposes wrongdoing or prompts needed change, I feel that I have the best job in the world.

What advice would you give to a journalism major?

Know what you want and want what you are good at. Then, don't take no for an answer. If it isn't in your soul, it won't be worth your blood, sweat and tears.

What would you tell yourself at the beginning of your career, if you could go back in time?

That I wanted to be a journalist and not an architect. That I had the raw talent and I should just have fun doing it. Life's short and there's just so much to see and do. Do it.

Chapter 10
Business Reporting

Courtesy of Clement H. Murray

There are two ways to approach business reporting. The first is with fear, as in "Oh my God! I don't know anything about business or numbers! I can barely balance my checkbook."

The second is to see business journalism as a great opportunity, with fascinating stories. Because it is.

Almost every topic can be made into a business story. High prices at the gas pump could turn into a business feature about a local gas station owner. A shortage of the flu vaccine at the county health department could inspire an investigation of the companies who manufacture the vaccine. A close friend's bankruptcy could lead to an examination of the new federal bankruptcy laws.

Business reporting may seem daunting because it deals with money – a very serious and complicated subject for most people. But once a reporter gets the hang of certain terms, jargon and resources, the business beat is manageable and interesting.

It can also be a lucrative beat. While many newspapers and magazines are downsizing their employees or offering buyouts, business reporters often keep their jobs and stand a better chance of finding another. Talented and skilled business reporters are usually in high demand at publications and wire services across the country. Plus, business reporters almost never have to cover murders (except in the economic sense).

Almost every part of daily life can be translated into a business story. Annoyed with your cable television selection? Write a story on the cable company in your area. Obsessed with your new computer? Profile the computer company CEO. Drowning in credit card debt? Follow a local couple who are using a debt consolidation company.

Supply and demand. Buy low and sell high. Follow the money. All those aphorisms apply to business reporting.

Many new reporters to the business beat get intimidated by the jargon. Words and phrases like "indexing" and "amortization" sound daunting. There are many good reference books for business journalists, so buy some and keep a stack at your office.

Here are some helpful titles: "Barron's Dictionary of Finance and Investment Terms," "Dictionary of Business Terms" and "Dictionary of Accounting Terms."

If you don't know what something means, don't be afraid to ask. Even if it seems stupid! It is much better to ask a question ahead of time than to make a stupid mistake in print or online.

Remember, reporters are not supposed to be experts in everything – they are supposed to be experts in finding out the answers to things.

Business people are savvy. Sometimes they are using big words and phrases simply because they WANT to obfuscate things. Again, ask them to explain, ask another source or go look it up.

If an issue or concept feels completely overwhelming, find some experts to help you. Business professors at local colleges and universities can be a great resource. So are stock analysts (if the company is publicly held) or simply other business people in town.

Here are some perennial story ideas for the business beat:

- The hottest **Christmas toy** for kids. Remember Cabbage Patch dolls? And Tickle Me Elmo?

- **Clothe**s. Check out what teenagers and young people are wearing, from low-cut pants to the return of bell bottoms. Whoever is making the clothes and selling them is making money.

- **Gas** prices. Up or down.

- **Food** prices. Up or down. Storms in California and Florida, for example, can affect produce prices. Go to the supermarket to check the cost of oranges and tomatoes.

- **New businesses** in town. Check out the new restaurants, novelty stores and donut shops.

- **Vehicles**. What car is everyone in your town driving?

- **Development**. Which business person or company wants to buy the vacant lot downtown and what do they plan to do with it?

- **Salaries.** What do the company executives in your town get paid?

Three Abbreviations/Acronyms to Know

Dow Jones

The Dow Jones is an indicator of the stock market, based on the averages of 30 blue-chip stocks on the New York Stock Exchange. Business people and reporters watch the Dow Jones because it is one of the best indicators of how the stock market is doing. It is often abbreviated to "the Dow," as in "the Dow is up today."

NASDAQ

The NASDAQ was the world's first electronic stock market. It is a computerized system that provides quick quotations on the stock market. Some of the biggest technology stocks, such as Microsoft and Intel, are traded on the NASDAQ.

SEC and EDGAR:

The SEC is supposed to act as the nation's financial watchdog. The agency collects a massive number of information and reports that publicly-traded companies are required to submit, and those documents are available to the general public via a free online service called EDGAR. (It can be found at www.sec.gov/edgar.shtml, and has a useful tutorial for first-time users.)

The SEC investigates charges of financial fraud and other white-collar crimes, and has the power to levy civil fines against individuals and corporations who break the rules. They can also forward cases to the Justice Department for criminal prosecution.

The unraveling of Enron, for example, began with an SEC investigation in at the agency's branch office in Fort Worth, Texas. It ended with Ken Lay and Jeffrey Skilling facing years in prison after being convicted in federal court on multiple charges.

For reporters, the SEC's primary value lies in the EDGAR database. The documents filed there can provide a fairly complete picture of a company's finances, everything from how much money it made or lost in the most recent quarter to how much the CEO is paid and whether the company kicked in for his country club membership last year. It also can provide tidbits like whether top executives are dumping their own company's stock or if worrisome lawsuits have been filed.

Journalist Stacy Jones planned on being a hard news reporter when she graduated from the University of Maryland with a master's degree in journalism. She covered news as an intern at both the Lakeland Ledger and USA Today. But an opening on the business desk at the Star-Ledger newspaper in Newark, NJ intrigued her. She got the job – her first out of graduate school – and realized she really enjoys the business beat. Here is her story:

Business section bylines don't require you to labor under a green eyeshade, calculate figures until your fingers bleed or crank out painfully dull stories.

Being open to tackling a business beat helped me land a job at New Jersey's biggest daily paper, The Star-Ledger, a couple of months after I finished my master's degree at the University of Maryland.

I had never, through internships or part-time jobs, been a business reporter before this job. So the last year has been a bit of a crash course.

I've treated it like a personal challenge to find the human stories behind otherwise bland, two-dimensional numbers. When an international trade report told me that New Jersey had been exporting a lot of products for medical and pharmaceutical companies, I found the owner of a pallet company in Trenton.

It was true. His company had lost accounts with food and machinery manufacturers after they went bankrupt and was instead buying new machines that could package chemicals in ultra-sterile plastic pallets. Wood is too messy.

Writing business stories means figuring out how statistics – no matter how reputable the source – come to exist.

I receive at least five business "surveys" or "reports" each day. You'd be surprised how many of them make broad claims with very little evidence to back them up. Or have been paid for by the very industries that they shower with praise.

The same innate desire to educate readers and call people on their dishonesty – or homework assignment – that brought you to this page will sing with joy when you can confidently chuck a misleading report and save your readers from another empty numbers story.

Yes, there are challenges to writing business stories. Don't expect to breeze through your first earnings report or piece of tax legislation. They can be tough to digest, but it gets easier with time. Simply familiarizing yourself with business terms will make you more confident. If you're a little self-conscious, Google the difference between an affiliate and a subsidiary from at home or on your phone.

Your inbox and voicemail will be a magnet for business owners who want – and feel they're entitled to – free advertising by way of a quote in your story. Or worse yet, they might expect a full-fledged feature in your business section.

Practice very sternly telling PR flaks that you get hundreds of pitches from businesses every day and can't possibly write about them all. But don't discount them entirely.

My first front page story at the Ledger came to be because I took the bait on a local soup manufacturer – a family business that had been selling its soups for generations. The press release glossed over something called Nutty Butta, a side project of the company's owner.

After visiting the plant and talking to Ben Tabatchnick about the Nutty Butta, I realized that was my story. Nutty Butta is a therapeutic food that's been used to save millions of children across the globe from famine. As the story went to print, the company had just won a contract to ship 500 metric tons of it to humanitarian workers in Somalia. It was the height of the horrific famine in the Horn of Africa that claimed tens of thousands of lives, most of them children.

Finally, you can't beat the hours. Unless you've always dreamed of earning your stripes chugging coffee during a night cops shift — and there's nothing wrong with that — you'll find that covering business means working largely during regular business hours.

I start at 11 a.m., after a mostly traffic-less commute, and head home most nights around 7 p.m. Good news: It seems most business people follow an unwritten rule of holding meetings and conferences during daylight hours. Aside from Black Friday and one man-on-the-street assignment at a grocery store, I haven't had to work at night.

If you're still not convinced you should give business reporting a shot, take a gander at some of the interesting assignments I've received just in my first year:

- *Economic impact of winning an Oscar for films*

- *Fake Christmas trees vs. real Christmas trees in consumer spending*

- *Heartbreaking dispatches from trash hauling companies that cleaned up debris from Hurricane Irene*

- *New Jersey toy companies at the 2012 International Toy Fair in NYC*

- *Cremations pulling almost even with burials as funeral preference*

- *Announcement of the Grand Prix of America, a Formula 1 race slated for NJ in 2013*

10 Tips on *Business Reporting*

- **Shake some hands.** Figure out what companies/businesses are on your beat and go meet the people involved. Schmooze the PR folks. Pass your card around the executive suite. Then come back the next day and do the same thing in the employee parking lot, where you'll meet the regular folks who work there. Remember that many employees should only be used on background rather than quotes, because they will worry about protecting their jobs.

- **Read the trade publications.** Nearly every beat has one or more trade publications that focus on that industry. Read them. When in doubt, read the Wall Street Journal.

- **Find the experts.** Most industries, and many individual companies, are monitored by independent experts. Find the experts who are knowledgeable about your beat, and talk to them regularly. Many of them are eager to be quoted, while others will insist on background conversations only. They are vital sources of independent information.

- **Scour the documents.** The business world is heavily regulated, and reams of public documents exist that can provide insight and stories ideas about companies, industries and corporate issues. Find the documents – on websites like EDGAR, in courthouses and in state capitals. Use them in stories.

- **Remember your audience.** A business reporter can easily get swept up in covering powerful people and companies and become immersed in the jargon and lingo. But don't forget that most publications are geared toward a general audience. Keep that in mind when writing and reporting.

- A business reporter is **paid to shop.** Seriously. Trips to the mall, supermarket and night spots are all fodder for business story ideas. If people are buying it, wearing it or eating it, the subject is a possible story topic.

- **Get the details right.** Good business writing is like good sports writing. The audience cares about the details. Business reporters need to present stories that are fresh and educational. Tell the audience something they didn't know before. But make sure to get the details right, because business people will know and they will care.

- **Get to know your community.** The complaint from many readers is journalists don't understand their concerns. Take time to understand your beat. If your job is to cover a furniture manufacturer, visit the factory. Get to know the workers. What are the workers' fears? Hopes? Opportunities?

- **Avoid being spun.** Understand the motive of the people who are talking to you, and be sure to spend time talking to sources who have no stake in the subject. They will be able to provide a more objective context.

- **Local = Global.** The late politician Thomas P. "Tip" O'Neill famously said, "All politics is local." All journalism is local, too. And global. Events occurring around the world could affect businesses in your community. Trade talks in Mexico might mean the biggest employer in your town is about to go out of business. Hurricane Katrina caused gas prices to skyrocket in the summer of 2005, even in places in the United States that were thousands of miles away from Louisiana.

In-Class Activity/Homework

1. Go to the grocery store. How much does it cost to buy peanut butter, jelly, bread and paper plates using brand name products? Now do the same with store brands. Now try it with generic brands.

2. Look up the stock symbol for a technology company (like Apple) or an oil company (like Exxon). How much does the stock cost per share? How much did it cost one year ago? Five years ago? How much money would you have earned or lost if you had bought the stock five years ago?

Journalist Q&A

Courtesy of Lauren J. Young

Bob King

Where do you work?
Politico

What is your beat or job title?
Deputy energy editor

Where did you go to college and what was your degree?
Penn State University. Bachelor of arts in journalism; minor in science, technology and society.

Did you work on your college newspaper or online news website?
Yes – four years on the staff of The Daily Collegian.

Did you have any internships? If so, where and what did you do?
Three internships: 1) Police reporting/feature writing, Bucks County Courier Times. 2) Copy editing, Middletown Times Herald-Record, Middletown, N.Y. 3) Business reporting, The Phoenix Gazette, Arizona.

When and where was your first journalism job? What is one thing you learned from it?
Copy editing, Sarasota Herald-Tribune in Sarasota, Fla. Never trust the police to spell anybody's name correctly or a funeral home to calculate anybody's age accurately.

What was the hardest part of your first journalism job?
Getting the paper out on time while dealing with reporters who hated answering copy editors' questions, line editors who didn't like to edit, difficult paste-up people* in the backshop who never followed instructions on how to lay out the pages, and a computer system that crashed all the time. [*Unfortunately, these people no longer exist at newspapers. Many of them were actually really great to work with.]

Many beginning journalists get very nervous about their first assignments. Did you get nervous and how did you cope?

Sometimes. I obsessively make lists – sources to keep in touch with and all their contact information; court cases I need to keep track of, etc.

What is the worst part about being a journalist?

It's often difficult to balance doing your job with enjoying the rest of your life (especially if you also enjoy your job and are trying to do it well). Non-journalists never understand why your schedule is so insane.

What is the best part?

You pretty much have free rein to learn more about any topic you find interesting.

What advice would you give to a journalism major?

Definitely get as many internships as you can – nothing beats working alongside actual journalists who do this every day for a living.

What would you tell yourself at the beginning of your career, if you could go back in time?

Take more biology and history classes.

Every journalist should read, learn and follow the Code of Ethics as set forth by the Society of Professional Journalists. The complete code is reprinted here, and can be accessed on the SPJ website, spj.org/ethicscode.asp

SPJ Code of Ethics

Preamble

Members of the Society of Professional Journalists believe that public enlightenment is the forerunner of justice and the foundation of democracy. The duty of the journalist is to further those ends by seeking truth and providing a fair and comprehensive account of events and issues. Conscientious journalists from all media and specialties strive to serve the public with thoroughness and honesty. Professional integrity is the cornerstone of a journalist's credibility. Members of the Society share a dedication to ethical behavior and adopt this code to declare the Society's principles and standards of practice.

The SPJ Code of Ethics is voluntarily embraced by thousands of journalists, regardless of place or platform, and is widely used in newsrooms and classrooms as a guide for ethical behavior. The code is intended not as a set of "rules" but as a resource for ethical decision-making. It is not — nor can it be under the First Amendment — legally enforceable.

Seek Truth and Report It

Journalists should be honest, fair and courageous in gathering, reporting and interpreting information.

Journalists should:

- Test the accuracy of information from all sources and exercise care to avoid inadvertent error. Deliberate distortion is never permissible.

- Diligently seek out subjects of news stories to give them the opportunity to respond to allegations of wrongdoing.

- Identify sources whenever feasible. The public is entitled to as much information as possible on sources' reliability.

- Always question sources' motives before promising anonymity. Clarify conditions attached to any promise made in exchange for information. Keep promises.

- Make certain that headlines, news teases and promotional material, photos, video, audio, graphics, sound bites and quotations do not misrepresent. They should not oversimplify or highlight incidents out of context.

- Never distort the content of news photos or video. Image enhancement for technical clarity is always permissible. Label montages and photo illustrations.

- Avoid misleading re-enactments or staged news events. If re-enactment is necessary to tell a story, label it.

- Avoid undercover or other surreptitious methods of gathering information except when traditional open methods will not yield information vital to the public. Use of such methods should be explained as part of the story

- Never plagiarize.

- Tell the story of the diversity and magnitude of the human experience boldly, even when it is unpopular to do so.

- Examine their own cultural values and avoid imposing those values on others.

- Avoid stereotyping by race, gender, age, religion, ethnicity, geography, sexual orientation, disability, physical appearance or social status.

- Support the open exchange of views, even views they find repugnant.

- Give voice to the voiceless; official and unofficial sources of information can be equally valid.

- Distinguish between advocacy and news reporting. Analysis and commentary should be labeled and not misrepresent fact or context.

- Distinguish news from advertising and shun hybrids that blur the lines between the two.

- Recognize a special obligation to ensure that the public's business is conducted in the open and that government records are open to inspection.

Minimize Harm

Ethical journalists treat sources, subjects and colleagues as human beings deserving of respect.

Journalists should:

- Show compassion for those who may be affected adversely by news coverage. Use special sensitivity when dealing with children and inexperienced sources or subjects.

- Be sensitive when seeking or using interviews or photographs of those affected by tragedy or grief.

- Recognize that gathering and reporting information may cause harm or discomfort. Pursuit of the news is not a license for arrogance.

- Recognize that private people have a greater right to control information about themselves than do public officials and others who seek power, influence or attention. Only an overriding public need can justify intrusion into anyone's privacy.

- Show good taste. Avoid pandering to lurid curiosity.

- Be cautious about identifying juvenile suspects or victims of sex crimes.

- Be judicious about naming criminal suspects before the formal filing of charges.

- Balance a criminal suspect's fair trial rights with the public's right to be informed.

Act Independently

Journalists should be free of obligation to any interest other than the public's right to know.

Journalists should:

- Avoid conflicts of interest, real or perceived.

- Remain free of associations and activities that may compromise integrity or damage credibility.

- Refuse gifts, favors, fees, free travel and special treatment, and shun secondary employment, political involvement, public office and service in community organizations if they compromise journalistic integrity.

- Disclose unavoidable conflicts.

- Be vigilant and courageous about holding those with power accountable.

- Deny favored treatment to advertisers and special interests and resist their pressure to influence news coverage.

- Be wary of sources offering information for favors or money; avoid bidding for news.

Be Accountable

Journalists are accountable to their readers, listeners, viewers and each other.

Journalists should:

- Clarify and explain news coverage and invite dialogue with the public over journalistic conduct.
- Encourage the public to voice grievances against the news media.
- Admit mistakes and correct them promptly.
- Expose unethical practices of journalists and the news media.
- Abide by the same high standards to which they hold others.

The SPJ Code of Ethics is voluntarily embraced by thousands of writers, editors and other news professionals. The present version of the code was adopted by the 1996 SPJ National Convention, after months of study and debate among the Society's members.

Sigma Delta Chi's first Code of Ethics was borrowed from the American Society of Newspaper Editors in 1926. In 1973, Sigma Delta Chi wrote its own code, which was revised in 1984, 1987 and 1996.

Recommended Reading List

Journalists become good reporters through talent, time and practice. Journalists become good writers in the same way, but also benefit from reading good writing. Here are some textbooks and non-fiction books that helped me as a journalist. I hope you might benefit from reading them, too.

Melvin Mencher. "News Reporting and Writing." 12th edition. McGraw-Hill. 2011. This book is the ultimate tome in journalism education, written by Mencher, a longtime newsman and Columbia University journalism professor. This classic text has almost everything you need to know about news and then some.

Chip Scanlan. "Reporting and Writing." Harcourt College Pub. 2000. Scanlan, a newspaper reporter for nearly 30 years, wrote this book in 2000 but much of its content is still relevant and extremely useful. Scanlan's chapters on lead writing and narrative elements are especially strong.

"Telling True Stories: A Nonfiction Writers' Guide from the Nieman Foundation at Harvard University." Edited by Mark Kramer and Wendy Call. Plume. 2007. More than 50 of journalism's best-known and most-talented writers contributed to this book. They present their best advice on finding a topic, doing research and telling a narrative story.

H. G. Bissinger. "Friday Night Lights: A Town, a Team and a Dream." Da Capo Press. 2000. This is the book about the high school football team in Texas that inspired the movie and television series of the same name. It's a classic in narrative nonfiction.

Ron Suskind. "A Hope in the Unseen." Broadway. 1999. This is the story about Cedric Jennings, a black student from a poor inner-city neighborhood in Washington, D.C. who excels and achieves, making his way to the Ivy League halls of Brown University. Suskind won a Pulitzer Prize for his series of articles in the Wall Street Journal that led to the book.

Rick Bragg. "All Over But the Shoutin'." Vintage. 1998. Rick Bragg, a Pulitzer Prize-winning feature writer, focuses on his hardscrabble childhood in Alabama in this memoir, and his journalism journey to the New York Times.

**Deborah Copaken Kogan. "Shutterbabe: Adventures in Love and War."
RandomHouse. 2002.** A memoir of photojournalist Kogan's experiences in
Paris and in conflict zones in Afghanistan, Zimababwe and Romania, with a
dash of romance and heartache along the way.

Edna Buchanan. "The Corpse Had a Familiar Face." Pocket. 2004.
The longtime police reporter at the Miami Herald, Buchanan explains and
explores the crazy crimes that people commit and why they do it.

Ted Conover. "Newjack: Guarding Sing Sing." Vintage. 2001.
Nonfiction writer went undercover as a prison guard at New York's
notorious Sing Sing penitentiary to shed light on the corrections system.

**Adrian Nicole LeBlanc. "Random Family: Love, Drugs, Trouble and
Coming of Age in the Bronx." Scribner. 2004.** Journalist LeBlanc spent
10 years following three Latina women and their families in this book,
which explores the realities of drug abuse, teen pregnancy and welfare.

**Kristen Mulvihill and David Rohde. "A Rope and a Prayer: A
Kidnapping from Two Sides." Viking Adult. 2010.** When Rohde,
a foreign correspondent from the New York Times was kidnapped in
Pakistan, his newlywed wife had to cope with his absence while trying to
keep his capture out of the media to protect his safety. This book alternates
between their separate experiences and culminates with Rohde's brave
escape to safety with his translator.

**Nicholas D. Kristof and Sheryl WuDunn. "Half the Sky: Turning
Oppression into Opportunity for Women Worldwide." Vintage. 2010.**
Journalists Kristof and WuDunn, who are also married, reported from
around the globe to bring to light a moral atrocity – the oppression of
females in the developing world.

Author's Note

This textbook is for journalism students everywhere, especially at Rowan University in Glassboro, NJ You inspire me every day with your energetic spirits, curious minds and challenging questions. Thank you for choosing the journalism profession, a path that can be equal parts rewarding and frustrating. The world needs good reporters and editors now more than ever and I hope this book helps you learn and grow.

Many thanks to my colleagues in the Journalism Department at Rowan. Claudia Cuddy, Carl Hausman, Candace Kelley and Mark Berkey-Gerard supported me, offered encouragement and filled in for me while I was on Sabbatical writing this book. More thanks to Deb Woodell, Amy Z. Quinn and Lisa B. Samalonis for being my sounding boards.

A number of dedicated and experienced journalists graciously contributed to this book. They include: Antigone Barton, Lisa L. Colangelo, Sue Livio, Bob King, Mary Ellen Flannery, Trymaine D. Lee, Stephen Stirling, Tanya Kenevich, Christina Paciolla, Jim Cook Jr., Brittany Wehner, Kristen Connor, Charles W. Nutt, Allie Harcharek, Dianna Cahn, Mike Boone, Stacy Jones, Kristen Graham, Rich Wisniewski, Cori Egan, Eliot Kleinberg, Kathy Bushouse Burstein and James Rosica. Thanks to Tom Scott for the great back cover photo.

Most of all, my deep gratitude to my fabulously talented layout editor, Nicole Reagan, and to my equally adept copy editor, Melissa Pileiro. I can't wait to see the places you go.

CPSIA information can be obtained
at www.ICGtesting.com
Printed in the USA
LVHW052227121120
671187LV00004B/21